A CONSERVATIVE
LOOKS AT COOPERATIVES

by Raymond W. Miller

OHIO   UNIVERSITY   PRESS,   ATHENS,   OHIO

334
M617c

We cross bridges built by others. The pages of this book are dedicated to two great 20th-Century "bridge builders of cooperation," EDWARD A. FILENE and HERBERT HOOVER. They spanned the chasms of economic frustration during the first half of this century that we may pass this way a little more easily. To them the free world owes an eternal debt.

FOREWORD

I first met Ray Miller in the student cafeteria of the Harvard Business School in 1948. Ray had just returned to Harvard from an overseas mission for the Food and Agriculture Organization of the United Nations. As a first-year student, I was fascinated by his reports of conversations with Prime Minister Nehru in India, Syngman Rhee in Korea, and Pope Pius at the Vatican.

Soon, I became a regular participant in the informal, highly-informative seminars which Ray gives every year at the Harvard Business School. Always timely, these seminars are geared closely to the pragmatic world of business. Ray has never lost touch with reality, yet he combines with his realism a deep humanity and a working code of ethics of the highest order.

In recent years, as Associate Dean of the Harvard Business School, I had the privilege of working closely with Ray on many projects of interest to the School involving business and government. President of Public Relations Research Associates, Inc. and World Trade Relations, Inc., a member of the Board of Trustees of American University, and a member of the Bar of the Supreme Court of the United States, Ray Miller has achieved success and respect in many circles. He is recognized as a businessman, an educator, a lawyer, and an expert on international affairs. A devout Methodist, Ray Miller would not be expected to have influence in the high councils of the Roman Catholic Church, but he does!

Private business ventures here and abroad have claimed a major portion of his time. Yet throughout his career, he has been a constant champion for the cooperative cause. Always his vision has been that cooperatives bring to their members that special initiative, health, and hope that one usually associates with arguments advocating capitalism. He carries the message everywhere that cooperatives are a natural and vital segment of a successful capitalistic private enterprise system. In many parts of the world, Ray Miller has had wide experience with cooperatives, and he presents the conclusion that they represent a step upward toward more "enlightened capitalism."

Here in *A Conservative Looks at Cooperatives* Ray Miller documents his beliefs and expands his message further. He argues well the cause for cooperatives.

This is a book with fresh thoughts and penetrating ideas. It deals with the further development and future opportunities for cooperatives. Ray Miller has been willing to examine the status quo, and he has suggested changes and new possibilities. He brings to the study of cooperatives deep convictions and unusual insights.

Since its founding in 1804, Ohio University has always supported new patterns in thought. As the first institution of higher learning in the Northwest Territory, Ohio University was on the frontier geographically in the last century and now, in this century, it is moving to the forefront academically. Its reputation as a pioneering institution is continuing. That the recently formed Ohio University Press should publish this book is appropriate because this is a work which explores the frontiers as well as the homeland of cooperatives. *A Conservative Looks at Cooperatives* fits well the basic mission and traditions at Ohio University.

VERNON R. ALDEN
President, Ohio University

6

In the years that I served as a Consultant to the Director General of the Food and Agriculture Organization of the United Nations, I was continually reminded of the material and spiritual ruin that has followed man's careless exploitation and wasteful use of this planet's natural resources. I became particularly aware of the carelessness and short-sighted policies that have led to the depletion of vast tracts of timber in many areas. I feel strongly, however, this is one natural resource that we can maintain and, indeed, nurture.

In 1955, while collaborating with the American Geographic Society in the publication of *A World Geography of Forest Reserves,* I became more convinced than ever that man must guard and preserve his natural resources as though his very life depended upon them—which, in truth, it does.

In practice—and I have seen these ideas borne out over the years in a tree farm which my family has operated on the Willamette River in Oregon—good forestry management can produce a constant supply of timber and pulp generation after generation, and at the same time provide for ample future supplies. The same basic theories of sound conservation and sensible management that we apply to our natural resources can be applied to other areas as well. During the twentieth century, a system of business, which I have termed "service capitalism," has developed in North America. The system is one in which capital performs a function for its owners by giving them a reasonable return on their investment, and for the community by performing certain needed services.

Within the area of service capitalism there are many types of businesses, just as there are many species of trees in the forests. Generally, however, we can distinguish three major divisions of capitalistic enterprise: profit and loss businesses, co-operative units, and state capitalism. The first two segments are basically beneficial to the community, but the last—that of

7

the state—should be held in reserve and used only when the other two have failed to perform their functions properly, or when the job is too big for them to handle. Too often, however, state capitalism may produce an environment in which man becomes a mere statistical unit. Under service capitalism, he is the master of his own destiny. Particularly under those areas of service capitalism that follow cooperative principles is man fully a part of his economic world.

Therefore, as a person who believes in the conservation of all natural resources, I have come to the conclusion that the cooperative is one of the great conservers of the service capitalism system.

Alfred North Whitehead, the famous mathematician and philosopher, once said, "The art of progress is to preserve order amid change and to preserve change amid order." The capitalistic cooperative is one of the few instruments devised by man that can help him attain this philosophy. But no such instrument can exist as an abstract idea or an unapplied principle. It has long been my belief that every great movement is dominated by the influence of a great leader Henry G. Bennett, the former President of Oklahoma State University and Administrator of the Technical Cooperation Administration, was an example of this belief. In the days when Oklahoma was in the agonies of the "dust bowl" era, I came to know him, and through his inspiration gained many of my ideas about the conservation of natural and human resources. He believed that cooperatives helped to preserve both. A capsule condensation of his faith in these ideals was contained in a speech that Henry Bennett delivered at Utah State University in 1951. Speaking on "Cooperatives in a World of Conflicts," he said:

> The cooperative movement springs from the inherent desire of men to be free. It is a mechanism which enables men working together to achieve what they could not achieve working singly and alone.

In summary, my belief is that a conservative is one who recognizes the need for sensible utilization of the resources available, and that a cooperative is an instrument through which a greater distribution of ownership can be maintained. Cooperatives and conservatives are ideological twins. Cooperatives, by definition, are at the furthest reach from statism; and conservatives, when faced by economic and social problems, try to solve them in voluntary joint effort, going to the government for help only as a last resort.

An example of this self-help procedure occurred many years ago in Sweden. A cartel controlled the manufacture of electric light bulbs and the prices seemed unreasonably high. After lengthy discussions, a cooperative built and put into operation its own light bulb manufacturing plant. Because of the competition which resulted, the cartel was forced to lower its prices and the entire community benefited. The citizens of Sweden had solved a problem through their own voluntary organization without resorting to the socialistic approach of "let the government do it."

My hope is that this book will serve as a statement of my belief that cooperatives are conservative organizations dedicated to individual ownership and to the principles of efficient and enlightened operation.

RAYMOND W. MILLER

Washington, D. C.
January, 1964

Contents

A CONSERVATIVE

LOOKS AT COOPERATIVES

I. One Man's Look at Cooperatives

"I have been a member of many cooperatives. I have studied them at home and abroad, watching some prosper and seeing some fail. I have seen the Soviet propaganda machine try to convince the world that its system encourages cooperatives —which it does not. It destroys them. I have seen cooperatives in many parts of the world where, in addition to being developers of individual initiative, they are supporting political liberty by demonstrating economic liberty."

How I Became a Convert

"Ray, why are you such a true believer in cooperatives?"

This question, in one form or another, has been asked me literally thousands of times. Usually the questioner is some person I have come to know in the ordinary pursuits and occupations of life, in business, on the university campus, or at church. Perhaps the questioner is some person with whom I happen to be traveling on a train or plane, someone I have engaged in casual conversation. Occasionally someone puts it in a more concrete form, such as, "Mr. Miller, cooperatives are socialistic, and meant to lead us down the rosy path to communism. How can you espouse them at the same time that you believe in our private enterprise system?"

Well, how did I become a convert to the cause of cooperatives? It was very simple and goes back to just after World War I. I had received my discharge from the army, and Mrs. Miller and I were already married. With only a couple of thousand

15

A Conservative Looks At Cooperatives

dollars between us, we signed mortgage papers and bought a
farm in California. The area was just then beginning to produce
walnuts as a minor crop.

Mrs. Miller and I levelled our land, planted the black nuts
in the ground, and then grafted the trees a few years later.
When the trees began to produce we marketed our nuts through
the California Walnut Growers Association, which is now the
Diamond Walnut Growers Association. We gave very little
thought at the time as to how to market our crop.

In 1930, I was President of the San Joaquin County Farm
Bureau. It so happened that, through the efforts of a fine group
of associates, our membership became the largest of any county
group in the United States. To our delight, we found that the
presiding officer of such a leading group was automatically
rewarded with a trip to the national convention of the American Farm Bureau. So it was that in 1930 Mrs. Miller and I
made our first trip together out of California and traveled to
Boston. I addressed the assembled delegates there, telling them
how our membership had grown. This was my first experience
as an active participant in a conference dealing with larger
problems than just those of my own county or state.

Mr. Charles Teague, President at that time of the California Walnut Growers Association, was one of the members
of the National Farm Board, which was then in its heyday. He
attended the American Farm Bureau meeting and a luncheon
was held at which the California delegates could visit with Mr.
Teague and other members of the Farm Board.

Mr. Teague reminisced for a couple of hours on the growth
of cooperatives in California and pointed out that because of
their cooperatives the California producers of specialty crops
were the only ones in the nation able to realize a decent return
on their products in this period of agricultural depression. Pecan
growers, for instance, who were direct competitors of walnut
producers, were getting only a "poverty return" for their labors.
As he spoke, I became increasingly aware of the tremendous

potential in this movement which I had only so recently taken for granted.

Since then, I have been a member of many cooperatives. I have studied them at home and abroad, watching some prosper and seeing some fail. I have seen the Soviet propaganda machine try to convince the world that its system encourages cooperatives—which it does not. It destroys them. I have seen cooperatives in many parts of the world where, in addition to being developers of individual initiative, they are supporting political liberty by demonstrating economic liberty.

As President and General Counsel of the American Institute of Cooperation (1945-1948), I had the unique opportunity, with Kelsey Gardner, then Principal Economist, Farm Credit Administration, U. S. Department of Agriculture, and Walter Bradley, CPA and Chairman, Committee on Cooperatives, American Institute of Accountants, of holding seventy-five clinics with a total attendance of over ten thousand directors and managers of cooperatives in the United States.

As a member of the Bar and friend of the court, I attended the sittings of the Royal Commission in Canada, which investigated the place of cooperatives in its economy. As consultant to the Director General of the Food and Agriculture Organization of the United Nations, it was my privilege to help develop the official statement made by the Director General, committing that organization to work with cooperatives. As a member of the faculty of the Harvard Graduate School of Business Administration, I participated in the development of its program of Agribusiness. As a member of various advisory committees to the Point Four Program and several nongovernmental organizations engaged in international affairs, I have seen the part that cooperatives play in the development of the philosophy of a free world for free men.

I hope the subsequent pages will present cases and evidence to help the reader understand the philosophy and usefulness of the nonprofit corporate entity. The nonprofit corporate entity is a definite part of the profit world, because its purpose is *to help its member patrons realize an individual profit or a saving through its use.* At the same time, through experience gained in the practical operation of economic democracy, its member patrons are better prepared to understand and participate in political democracy.

Herbert Hoover's Evaluation of and Prophecy for Co-operatives—1922

In 1934, I first became acquainted personally with Herbert Hoover. Since then, I have valued our friendship, and we have had an exchange of many ideas. I found that Herbert Hoover not only believed in cooperatives but had, in 1922, written a 72-page booklet, *American Individualism,* in which he expressed in unequivocal terms his faith in them as part and parcel of American capitalism.

Because the following paragraph is one of the keenest analyses ever written on the place of the nonprofit corporation in the economy of freedom, I asked his permission to use it in this book. He immediately and enthusiastically granted this permission, and it is presented herewith as being, in my judgment, the manifesto of Cooperatives:

> Today business organization is moving strongly toward cooperation. There are in the cooperative great hopes that we can even gain in individuality, equality of opportunity, and an enlarged field for initiative, and at the same time reduce many of the great wastes of over-reckless competition in production and distribution. Those who either congratulate themselves or those who fear that cooperation is an advance toward socialism need neither rejoice nor worry. Cooperation in its current economic sense represents the initiative of self-interest blended with a sense of service, for nobody belongs to a cooperative who is not striving to sell his products or services for more or striving to buy from others for less or striving to make his income more secure. Their members

are furnishing the capital for extension of their activities just as effectively as if they did it in corporate [*profit* — Ed.] form and they are simply transferring the profit principle from joint return to individual return. Their only success lies where they eliminate waste either in production or distribution—and they can do neither if they destroy individual initiative. Indeed this phase of development of our individualism promises to become the dominant note of its twentieth-century expansion. But it will thrive only insofar as it can construct leadership and a sense of service, and so long as it preserves the initiative and safeguards the individuality of its members.[1]

This prophecy of Herbert Hoover has proven to be correct, not only for the United States, but for many other parts of the world.

My adaptation of Mr. Hoover's "landmark" statement, brought up-to-date by my own experience, is the theme of this book:

> Cooperatives are catalysts, which because of member participation, understanding, and experience, help make possible the development of a competitive, capitalistic economy with individual economic, political, judicial, and social liberties.
>
> Cartels, monopolistic-exploitative capitalism, produce the cataclysm, which, because of individual frustration thus created, makes probable the ascendancy of dictatorial communism. This, in turn, destroys or makes impossible competitive, capitalistic enterprise and economic, political, judicial, and social liberties.

I have used this evaluation of cooperatives before many audiences and their reaction, and that of the press covering these meetings, shows that there is an intense interest in this fundamental idea of cooperatives being the antithesis of monopolistic capitalism and its spawn—dictatorial communism.

[1]*Herbert Hoover,* American Individualism *(New York, 1922), pp. 44-45. Used with permission.*

A CONSERVATIVE LOOKS AT COOPERATIVES

TECHNICAL MEETING ON COOPERATIVES IN ASIA AND THE FAR EAST—1949

I presented further proof of the accuracy of Mr. Hoover's evaluation of the area of the cooperative on the map of freedom in *Can Capitalism Compete?*,[2] when I wrote:

> This problem was dramatically brought to my attention in October, 1949, when I was legal consultant to the Technical Meeting on Cooperatives of South East Asia at Lucknow, India. Representatives of the "new countries" of that area which were just "hatching" from under the hen of colonization met there in peace and harmony with representatives of the colonial powers. Japanese were on committees with Americans as representatives of the "occupying power." A New Zealander, Dr. Horace Belshaw, was the General Secretary representing the Food and Agriculture Organization of the United Nations. I was there as his and their adviser.
>
> Perhaps a person might pray that once in a lifetime he might reach a pinnacle experience in human relations. Well, I reached mine, and I have never come out from under its influence. Here were men whose people had just been through the greatest cataclysm in history. They were gathered together to work out a system of economic law and order under capitalism. The fear of these men was that cooperatives with individual capitalistic members might fall under the Soviet concept of "forced cooperatives," where just the name remained and whose function was the antithesis of the freedom of choice under the "true" cooperative. China, only a few hours away, was just rolling under the red carpet and these men knew that there, at least, capitalistic cooperatives would never now be tried. They were up against the hard facts of reality, and as events turned out were better prophets than many of the forecasters.

[2]*Raymond W. Miller*, CAN CAPITALISM COMPETE? *(New York, 1959), p. 62.*

II. The Philosophy and Functions of Cooperatives

"Only in a land of free men can citizens join a voluntary association of their own choosing. Cooperatives represent democratic principles applied to business."

"The cooperative, in improving and stabilizing members' income, has greatly increased their purchasing power and ability to patronize all business."

"Were it not for the cooperatives bringing the people's viewpoint into business, business as a whole would deteriorate to such a degree that ultimately communism would take it over."

THE PLACE OF A COOPERATIVE CORPORATE ASSOCIATION IN A DEMOCRACY

Democracy is a form of government wherein individuals have retained certain rights, liberties, privileges, and immunities, and, *ipso facto,* accepted corresponding duties as responsible citizens.[1]

Representative democracy encourages procedure whereby the benefits of group research or action may accrue to the individual members of an organization. While government may often act as a conciliator or arbitrator, it has a direct interest in

[1]*This and the following paragraphs are from Raymond W. Miller,* THE FARM COOPERATIVE CORPORATE ASSOCIATION *(Washington, D. C., 1948). See also Joseph G. Knapp, "The Scope of Farmer Cooperatives,"* JOURNAL OF FARM ECONOMICS, *XLIV (May, 1962), 476.*

the conduct of all segments of the community which bear upon the general welfare. In order that group action may be in the public interest, governments authorize and encourage the formation of corporate entities so that the legal persons thus created shall be readily responsible to the state.

There are various types of corporations permitted by law: business and commercial for financial profit; ecclesiastical, to function in the restricted field of organized religion; eleemosynary, to execute works of charity in a progressive society; educational, to insure a nobler standard of human understanding and efficiency; and service, to promote and enhance a finer standard of living.

Business bodies corporate are roughly divided into two classifications. The first may be called private profit and loss corporations; the second, corporations not for profit. The private profit corporation expects to succeed entirely through dealings with third parties; businesses engaged in the wholesale and retail trade, manufacturing, processing and marketing, and public utilities belong to this category. The nonprofit form of private enterprise is created to perform services for its members and nonmember patrons at cost; the Associated Press and the Canadian Press, many mutual insurance companies, cooperative banks, credit unions, voluntary associations of retail stores, group hospitalization, and farmer cooperatives belong to this category. In fact, profit corporations often incorporate nonprofit entities to expedite and facilitate their own services, for example to make purchases for groups of retailers.

Legislative assemblies have recognized that farmers need the benefit of off-farm nonprofit selling and purchasing corporations to compete in the twentieth-century world of corporate business. The federal Capper-Volstead Act of 1922 and state corporation statutes have accordingly been enacted enabling farm groups to carry on business activities for the benefit of the individual farmer and in the interest of the general welfare.

Dr. A. Ladru Jensen, Professor of Corporation Law at the

University of Utah, has pointed out that the cooperative non-profit corporation constitutes a unique blending of corporate entity with a member association. He says:

> A cooperative marketing corporation is the only business unit in which the members of the corporation form a large production association of individual enterprisers. The members are associated together by the legal device of identical marketing contracts which obligate each member of the corporation to use the corporate entity as his marketing and often purchasing agent, and which also obligate the corporation to market each member's agricultural products, and frequently to purchase farm supplies, without any profit to itself. This explains why nearly all state statutes designate this type of business unit as a "cooperative corporation association."

Must Meet Specific Requirements

Cooperative associations are nevertheless corporations created under state statutes. In chartering any corporation, the government prescribes certain conditions prerequisite to organization, and, following incorporation, there are statutory conditions that must be met. Farmer cooperatives are no exception to these procedures and conditions. They are granted certain rights and privileges by the government and, correspondingly, acquire certain responsibilities and duties predicated upon their operating within the restrictions of their corporate charters. Cooperatives, like other corporations, pay such taxes as are prescribed by statute.

An incorporated cooperative is a legal entity with an objective and control different from that of most other corporations. The voting control of business corporations ordinarily is proportionate to money invested. The ultimate objective of the company is to make a profit out of dealings with third parties. Most cooperative corporate associations have the rule of one-member one-vote, regardless of capital investment or percentage of patronage. The objective is to make profit or savings for the members through use of their nonprofit corporate agent.

23

A Conservative Looks At Cooperatives

Satisfy Vital Economic Needs

A cooperative can and should implement a vital, economic need. It should not be started merely on the basis of local pride or desire. Careful study of the proposal for a new organization will avoid having several units competing for business capable of being handled by one organization. Those proposing the formation of a new cooperative should prove that existing commercial facilities and services are inadequate, unfair, or too costly.

To be successful and to serve its members effectively, a cooperative, whether of the marketing, purchasing, or related service type, must establish and conduct its operations so as to provide a realistic, practical service attuned to the requirements of its members. Its goal must not be merely the rendering of a much needed service but one that assures members an efficient and vigorous operation. Cooperative management must recognize the importance of rendering only those services it can perform efficiently and at a saving to its members.[2]

Serve Many Purposes

Cooperatives exist in many fields of the national economy. Some act as bargaining agents of individual farmers in securing markets without actually handling the product itself. Some maintain grading, classifying, and/or assembling facilities whereby the products of many farms are pooled and sold in uniform containers under established standards. Others further integrate the marketing function on the road to the consumer through extensive advertising, dealer service, and, in some cases, retail outlets—in all cases on a nonprofit basis to the corporation itself. A cooperative is merely the corporate service agency of the individual producer or consumer.

In the purchasing field, some cooperatives merely buy a

[2]*See also* Journal of Farm Economics, *XLIV, No. 2 (May, 1962), 275.*

product, such as lumber, fertilizer or feed, in quantity lots on behalf of and for distribution to their patrons. Others establish manufacturing plants whereby raw material is milled or fabricated into food, fertilizer or machinery ready for farm use. Still others drill wells, maintain refineries and pipe lines and produce synthetic "hay"—gasoline and oil—for the "iron horses" of the farm. In agriculture, the tendency is for farm people to integrate their business sufficiently to avoid buying retail and selling wholesale.

The cooperative has gone through its period of trial and error. It has often lacked efficient direction and managerial personnel, a membership educated in cooperative principles, and an appreciation and understanding of buyers or suppliers; but these conditions have been to a great extent remedied.

Appreciation Based on Understanding

Cooperatives are not a passing phase in the business world. They are here to stay and business should learn to understand them. With understanding will come appreciation. The cooperative movement will continue to grow at a moderate rate of speed. How fast the development will be, however, will be determined largely by the extent to which the business world appreciates and works with the movement. Cooperatives will not for the most part embark upon business ventures unless existing facilities are unsatisfactory.

Business too often has sold consumers those things that would return large profits on invested capital, or which satisfied the whim of some erratic sales manager or production engineer without an understanding of needs. Profit business should study the market and sell only high-quality products that meet a real need. The day when the farmer was thought of as an illiterate, trusting yokel ready to purchase a lightning rod with no connections or an inefficient piece of farm machinery gaudily painted is rapidly passing.

The "hick" farmer is an anachronism. There was a time

25

when farmers were sold sand for fertilizer and straw mixed with debris from the floors of grain elevators as concentrated dairy food. Short weights were common. The need for farmer cooperatives was indicated by the findings of a 1917 study by the State of New York Joint Legislative Committee on Dairy Products, Livestock and Poultry:

> A wide field for fraudulent operation exists in the selling of concentrated feeding stuffs to the dairymen of this state . . . which are shown upon analysis to contain a large amount of worthless material and are a fraud upon the dairyman who buys them. . . . It is not going too far to assert that many thousands of dollars are yearly paid out by the dairymen of the State of New York for dirt, dust, straw and rubbish, permitted to be sold under some high sounding name as a valuable cattle feed, sure to increase the production of his dairy.

While only a few business institutions practiced this charlatanism, based upon the gullibility of the rural citizen, there was too much of it and there still is a feeling on the part of some trade groups that there is an "open season" on consumers and that they may be "taken in" with impunity.

Cooperative entities and the farseeing profit and loss businesses over the years have developed activities and programs which help protect consumers from such exploitations. Scientific laboratories are carrying on intensive research to produce better products which will be marketed more efficiently.

The business community as a whole now accepts cooperatives. Business has seen that the cooperative acts as a stabilizing influence on the nation's economy. Moreover, the cooperative is democratic and representative in form.

Valued as Pacesetters

The cooperative acts as a yardstick and pacesetter for the economy as a whole. There are large areas in America where profit and nonprofit supply and marketing organizations oper-

26

ate in peace and good fellowship. There are others where the economic battle becomes bitter and personal. Fortunately, most executives of the profit world, and those of the nonprofit, are men of good judgment who have an abiding faith in the American way of doing things. They recognize that every type of business has a service to perform.

The intrinsic value of joint effort is evidenced by the fact that millions of farm families have entrusted billions of dollars of agricultural business to their own service organizations. The value of cooperatives as a part of economic existence is being demonstrated daily by thousands of efficiently operated customer-owned business concerns.

Help Stabilize National Economy

The worth of cooperatives to the nation as a whole cannot be too strongly emphasized. The cooperative, in improving and stabilizing members' income, has greatly increased the purchasing power of its membership. The result is more saving and greater production, both of which are reflected in larger purchases of supplies and living necessities and a more uniform supply as to quantity and quality for the consumer.

Members of those very few cooperatives which have failed to assume proper moral, social, and economic responsibility should insist on reorganization. Such action is imperative, not only for the families directly concerned, but for the cooperative as a unit.

In addition to the economic advantages of cooperative action, there are intangible but measurable spiritual results. The mere fact that families meet on a commodity or business basis to help one another in an economic way is reflected in an increased interest in those other virtues that are roughly defined by the term "spiritual." The great church organizations of the democratic countries appreciate and encourage the part that cooperatives play in building better men as well as in saving dollars.

A CONSERVATIVE LOOKS AT COOPERATIVES

Democracy in government can become more workable when there are groups of people within it using a cooperative method in dealing with one another.

Cooperatives have a tremendously increased opportunity to serve. Their members and officials should recognize more than ever that the authoritarian form of government countenances no cooperative effort. Only in a land of free men can citizens join a voluntary association of their own choosing. Cooperatives represent democratic principles applied to business. Cooperation and cooperators are two of the strongest bulwarks of stability for agriculture, industry, and government.

The 1962 *Yearbook* of the U.S. Department of Agriculture notes that "Cooperatives help to keep our free enterprise system competitive." This statement by Dr. Joseph G. Knapp tersely sums up the basic reason why this author believes in cooperatives as a vital part of the private enterprise system.

THE MAGIC OF COOPERATIVE EFFORT

Some years ago, Edward A. Filene decided to take a round-the-world trip for pleasure and relaxation. Mr. Filene was a very successful Boston merchant. His trip included a short stay in India. Filene had been alarmed at the poverty of many of the working men and women of the United States and was shocked at the high rates of interest charged them for necessity loans by the money lenders or loan sharks, as they are called in North America. However, no one had seemed able to bring forth an idea whereby these people could be helped, save by charity. He had learned, as many millions of others had, that subsidies and charities are only temporary in their benefits and often are worse than the economic disease itself. Self-help was of ancient origin but it seemed to have been unavailable to the working man and his family in dire need of money for emergencies. The loan shark had no sympathy. He charged all that was possible and the poor man was often so deeply in debt because of one small loan with excessive interest that he became a drag both on himself and society. Often he could only get out of debt by taking a new loan to pay off the original and its accumulated interest. Often debts were passed on to sons and daughters.[3]

In India, Filene came face to face, for the first time, with the answer to this problem. He was stunned and excited. He—Filene—had encountered the indigenous Credit Union—the poor man's bank. By a simple device of having people save as little as an anna each a week, a group of individuals accumulated enough to start a bank. He saw that the idea worked even though the directors of the small loan society could often neither read nor write. He learned what Rizal, the great Philippine Malay leader, had learned and taught, *viz.*, that intelligence has little to do with literacy; that education merely liberates intellect for use by man, selfishly or for the public welfare.

Filene abandoned his vacation trip and left almost immediately for the United States where he became the champion of the establishment of Credit Union institutions in his own land. For the remainder of his life he neglected his own business and became a crusader for the Credit Union idea. At first his fellow industrialists looked upon him as a crank. However, before he died he had demonstrated to great and small that when poor men borrowed at reasonable rates from their own institution and used this institution as a reservoir for their savings, a real contribution to society had been made. The idea was ripe for fruition and the growth of credit unions in the United States has been one of the marvels of modern finance. Their record of success has been even greater than that of the regular banking institution. The competition from these small unions soon brought the regular rates of money lenders down and lenders were compelled to follow suit. On the completion

[3] *This and the following paragraphs are from the article by Raymond W. Miller in* KURUKSHETRA *(Delhi, India, March 1, 1954).*

of the Russell Sage Foundation study which was inspired by Filene as a result of his Indian experience, the individual states were quick to pass protective legislation for the small borrower.[4]

Today the loan shark has all but vanished in the United States, and over 21 thousand credit unions in 1962 had total assets of over seven billion dollars—a monument to the vision of a great man.

The method of organizing a Credit Union is not patentable. All men, no matter where they live or what race they are, can avail themselves of the idea. Men have always worked together for self and community interest. The Credit Union is merely another exemplification of this basic human idea. The Credit Union does not depend upon the largess of government for its existence but allows the small man to be a self-respecting member of his society. It is the antithesis of statism and spoon-feeding.

Cooperatives are usually successful when they are built upon a common need with loyal and well-informed membership and when government nurtures their growth by creating a favorable climate. Cooperatives fail when there is too much interference from the government and when their membership is ill-informed.

Many successful cooperatives operate in the fields of credit, purchasing, and marketing. *The record of failures when ownership of the means of production is cooperative is very high. Where individual ownership is retained and the cooperative is used as a tool for service, the rate of success is extremely high. The cooperative is not a cure-all.*

Many people fail to recognize that a cooperative has all of the frailties of an ordinary profit and loss business. Others

[4]*The story of Mr. Filene's role in the development of the Credit Union cooperative idea is given in graphic terms in the following two books: Richard Y. Giles and Wallace J. Campbell,* Credit for the Millions *(New York, 1951); and Roy F. Bergengren,* Credit Union, North America *(New York, 1940).*

think that cooperatives should receive special subsidies and favors. Unfortunately these well-meaning individuals are usually disillusioned when their subsidized cooperative fails. A cooperative can only succeed when its membership assumes responsibility. Cooperatives must pay salaries to employees comparable to those paid by similar business undertakings, promptly repay loans, and not ask or expect special favors.

A cooperative can be of great help in building a free economy when it operates along the lines of responsible self-help. It should be looked upon as an agent of its members to do those things that they cannot economically do for themselves. The members themselves retain their own individual identities in their own producing units and use the cooperative as a marketing, credit, or purchasing service. When operated in such a manner, I know of no more valuable legal or economic tool in helping to advance the material welfare of a particular group.

ELECTRIC COOPERATIVES BRING BENEFITS

The rural electric associations have within a generation brought to people living on millions of farms and in thousands of villages and small towns the benefits of modern living. When the REA concept was first debated, there was a strong belief that rural communities could not afford the "luxury" of electricity. A great many people felt that the government would lose millions in loans to the rural cooperatives established to furnish electricity. In fact, many critics labeled the effort as a socialistic adventure.[5]

In the space of only a few years the whole picture has changed. The REA has made it possible for cooperative private

[5]This and the following paragraphs are from an address by Raymond W. Miller at the annual meeting of Rural Electric Associations of North Dakota, South Dakota, and Minnesota at Aberdeen, South Dakota, October 1, 1956.

enterprise to make power available to people living out where the creeks fork. New and wider uses for electricity in farm and rural communities have been developed.

Electric Service Enriches Lives of Rural People

In August, 1956, I attended the International Conference on the Church and Rural Life at the Ecumenical Institute in Bossey, Switzerland. Dr. Henry S. Randolph, of the Presbyterian Board of Missions, was among the principal discussion leaders and he presented a paper on "Special Problems Inherent in the Structure of Rural Society in the United States." This paper was one of the highlights of the meeting. Among the statements that he made was one which received special attention from various church leaders:

> Rural electrification has brought to the farmer many of the advantages of city living, such as better sanitation, better food preservation, and consequently better health. It has also lessened the amount of farm drudgery. Moreover, it has made possible the widespread use of radio and television, which connects the farmer directly to the cultural, political, social and industrial events and problems of the entire world.

Manufacturers of stoves and refrigerators and vacuum cleaners and radio and TV sets have been able to widen their sales and bring down the prices for all America because of the basic demand stemming from REA lines—a vast sales field not contemplated by market surveys of just a few years ago.

If the REA concept of cooperative ownership of electrical distribution facilities had not come into existence, it is probable that by now the rural community would have begun to have power, but it would have been provided by government-owned corporations. One can see this type of distribution in operation in Canada. REA is in a position to combine the efficiency of a profit-making organization with the services of a nonprofit enterprise, while at the same time keeping the whole operation in private rather than state ownership. Too few people, urban or rural, have realized the great national service that electric cooperatives have rendered.

Electric cooperatives are the balance wheel between private monopoly and government in business. Because private power companies under their present rate structures cannot serve the cooperatives' retail areas, the electric co-ops have provided the great middle ground—the bulwark of private ownership in the rural electric business.

Many people living in rural communities and benefiting from REA are so close to the situation that they lack the perspective to appreciate what REA has done for them. One of the tales of Tagore, the great Hindu poet and storyteller, illustrates the point. He described a young man who was told that on the beach there was a stone which, if held in the hand and touched to iron, would change the iron to gold. The lad secured an iron chain and, wearing it as a belt, began laboriously to search for the touchstone, picking up stones from the shore and touching each to the chain. Years rolled by, youth passed, then middle age. Old age came and he was still picking up stones. One day a youngster playing on the beach saw the old man and was fascinated to see the beautiful golden chain around his waist. "Where did you get the gold chain?" the child asked. The old man slowly bent his head to look at the bright circlet, realizing with a shock that sometime in the dim days of the past he had actually found the touchstone that turned iron to gold. He had been too busy gathering stones to notice!

The electric cooperatives have led America's rural people from the hard, drab, cold iron existence of the past into the golden, modern age of comfort and convenience. They have confounded their enemies and even amazed their friends. Their record of repayment to the government on borrowed money ranks among the best. Rural people pay their bills.

With the coming of electric current the way of life in

millions of homes has changed and electric appliances are today a part of the normal life of the ruralist.

PEOPLE TO PEOPLE

The Christian missionary from America traveled to the uttermost parts of the earth. He made few converts to the faith, but he brought with him the notion of social justice. To most people in strange lands, he was the first American they had ever seen. He built the first schools. He translated the oral language of the natives into a written form. He built gardens. By and large the missionary, educator, doctor, engineer, or agriculturist broke the "time barrier" of the centuries, and opened the minds and hearts of millions of men who had never even heard the story of the Gospel. Unfortunately, the traveling tradesmen and diplomats seldom got to the people. The missionary lived with them because he was there to help people. He lived "for" the people and not "off" them.[6]

In this connection, I present a significant quotation from an article in the April, 1958, issue of *Scouting* by Dr. Arthur A. Shuck, Chief Scout Executive, Boy Scouts of America, entitled "People to People Can Spell Peace":

> This fact was uppermost in the mind of President Dwight D. Eisenhower when in September, 1956, he called together a group of leading American citizens in a special White House conference in Washington, D. C., to discuss ways in which lasting two-way understanding could be established between Americans and citizens of other lands on a People-to-People—Person-to-Person basis as distinct from official government contact.

[6]*This and the following paragraphs are from "People to People — Industrial Relations — as the World Sees US," address by Raymond W. Miller at the annual meeting of the Foreman's Club of Reading and the Manufacturers Association of Berks County, Pennsylvania, March 27, 1958.*

I shall never forget the sincerity and forcefulness of President Eisenhower as he spoke to us at that meeting. With great feeling he said:

> "The purpose of this meeting is the most worthwhile purpose there is in the world today, namely—to help build a road to peace—to help build a road to an enduring peace."
>
> "The work we expect to do," he said, "is based on the assumption that no people, as such, want war—that all people want peace."
>
> "If we are going to take advantage of the assumption that all people want peace—then the problem is for people to get together to work out not one method but thousands of methods by which people can gradually learn a lot more of each other."

President Eisenhower added that the People-to-People Program is not an effort to induce other people to adopt American ways—economic, religious, or political. Rather it respects the belief that America can live as a good partner in the world with people of widely divergent cultural backgrounds—people who are trying to develop themselves peaceably, in accordance with their own particular heritages.

Man and Aspirations

Studies that Public Relations Research Associates, Inc., has made show that, fundamentally, the balanced life of man is predicated upon eight personal aspirations. They are:

1. To be loved
2. To belong
3. To participate
4. To be recognized in accomplishment
5. To be secure
6. To exercise freedom of choice
7. To attain status of dignity and honor
8. To freely practice one's faith or religion

A Conservative Looks At Cooperatives

These fundamental desires find expression in personal satisfactions and in awareness of the problems of others at home and abroad. However, man is not satisfied merely to have decency for himself. He wants it for others, too. Fred S. Bushmeyer of the National Council of Churches recently stated:

> We are the first generation in human history for whom it is literally true that there is neither safety nor salvation for any single group of people apart from a general concern for the safety and salvation of all the people throughout the world.

American Labor Understands

Acceptance of this philosophy toward world problems is indicated in the Statement on Foreign Economic Policy of the AFL-CIO Executive Council of February 8, 1958:

> The economic policy of the United States in the international arena must be attuned to the welfare and security of our own nation and the economic requirements and aspirations of the peoples of the Free World. Our leadership of the democratic forces of the world and our own national security require that in our economic policies the United States must not turn its back on the rest of the world.
>
> Americans must realize that we cannot build our own prosperity and security in economic isolation. In our economic no less than in our political decisions, we must recognize the growing interdependence of the peoples of the Free World. Economic cooperation among the nations of the Free World is essential to advance the welfare of humanity and to meet successfully the growing challenge of Soviet imperialism.
>
> The welfare of more than a billion people just beginning to aspire to a better life as well as the welfare and security of our own nation provide compelling reasons for the United States to improve and expand our program of assistance to underdeveloped areas.
>
> The assistance our country gives to fostering sound economic growth in underdeveloped countries can help

to strengthen freedom and democracy and weaken forces of Soviet totalitarianism. Unfortunately, we have been lagging in our foreign aid efforts while the Soviet rulers, utilizing foreign aid as an effective political weapon, have greatly expanded their financial commitments to underdeveloped areas.

We must meet this challenge by expanding our foreign aid program and gearing it to the needs and aspirations of the peoples of the underdeveloped areas.

The benefits of the economic development program should be widely shared by the peoples of the underdeveloped countries. In particular, positive encouragement should be given to the development of strong, democratic institutions in the underdeveloped countries, such as cooperatives and trade unions, as a fundamental part of the economic expansion program.

COOPERATIVES . . . CATALYSTS FOR FREEDOM IN THE COMMUNITY OF NATIONS

The American Institute of Cooperation is one of the most important organizations in the free world.[7] Its policy is not to enact resolutions but to call attention to various problems and developments in the area of its interests. It has been in existence for thirty-three years. These are some of the conclusions this organization has come to:

Cooperatives are voluntary organizations.

They are afflicted with all the business and managerial problems of other businesses, plus membership relations.

Cooperatives have often been born of adversity and deteriorate with prosperity. When cooperatives were born we were in the horse and buggy age. Rural areas were dominant politically.

[7]This material is from a presentation by Raymond W. Miller at the summer session, American Institute of Cooperation, University of California, August 8, 1960, published in AMERICAN COOPERATION, 1960 (American Institute of Cooperation, Washington, D. C.).

A Conservative Looks At Cooperatives

When farmer cooperatives began to be of major importance about the beginning of this century, they had little business efficiency. They were largely built on emotion—resentment against unfair trade practices of the petty kings of business.

Cooperatives were basically to fill a local need.

They were not consumer-minded.

They were violently anti-urban.

They were not quality-conscious.

The farm woman had little to do with them—like a lodge.

Problems Farmer Cooperatives Face In The Future

Now in the 1960's we have a new world.

Farmers are now a minority and are getting more so (about 9 percent).

In 1964 Congress will have at least one hundred fewer rural Congressmen than the Congress of a decade earlier and state legislatures follow the same trend.

There is great resentment against the "coddling of farmers."

Cooperatives are looked upon erroneously as tax evaders.

Rural youth is becoming educated.

Women are doing more and more of the purchasing—70 percent or more.

Controlled local markets are largely gone (transportation fluidity of people).

The local lodge is dead—dying or revamping.

The local church is substantially different.

The local store is often gone and a chain, corporate or voluntary, is in its place; the surviving local store is normally a member of a wholesale buying cooperative.

Cooperatives must consider the question of what is to be done about membership relations.

Loyalty is now based upon need plus efficiency.

Cooperatives must be made alluring to young people (too many young people want nothing to do with them).

Women should have a say based upon intelligence and ability.

Agricultural cooperatives will need alliances in the 1960's.

The Capper-Volstead and other agricultural cooperative enabling Acts cannot be defended by the few farmers alone.

Cooperatives should take a look at the consumer and must not be afraid of consumer cooperatives. In the 1960's and 1970's cooperatives must stick together.

What Do Successful Cooperative Managements Believe?

The cooperatives that have survived and prospered have recognized that:

Change is the law of life.

Management must manage.

Research is as necessary as insurance.

Membership must be informed through service, not alone by publicity.

Public relations is everybody's business.

Knowledge and love of agriculture do not necessarily assure good business judgment.

Cooperatives must compete in the market place, but must be member-centered.

The modern farm wife is knowledgeable as to economics.

The present leaders will be gone in the twenty-first century and their successors are now being groomed.

Employment of good brains by a cooperative must be so rewarding that sons of present cooperators will aspire to such activity and not all have a desire for a city or professional career.

Television, radio, and press are all-important in informing members and the public, but there is no substitute for a loyal family whose loyalty is based upon experience.

Cooperatives should never get too big to be a "swapping" center for ideas of members. Most ideas for human betterment come from the individual of "low estate" who is concerned

with freedom, justice, and human dignity. The effectiveness of
nonprofit businesses must be based upon *Education, Participation* and *Concern*—the passwords to cooperatives.

Three Major Steps for Future Success

If farmer cooperatives are to survive and serve, they must
adjust to bi-focal planning, both for short-run and long-run survival. Among other programs, they should consider:

1. *Electing a qualified woman to the board of directors of
every federated and regional cooperative and on many locals.*
Competitors in the food, textile, and service field have elected
women directors to their boards, and find that it pays off. As
an example, General Foods has found its woman director of great
value. The American Institute of Cooperation has a woman,
Mabel Robinson, as Assistant Secretary-Treasurer.

2. *Creating a "multiple" junior management board of directors chosen from the younger members.* Commercial industry
has proven the value of this practice. By "multiple management"
is meant a board which meets prior to the regular board and discusses the same agenda and has its findings considered by the
legally responsible board. The practice combines the enthusiasm
of youth and the experience of age. Cooperators spend much
time and money on youth, but give them little place in counseling.

3. *Recognizing that cooperative business has been substantially endorsed by nearly all Christian faiths.* There is something
about cooperative theory that ties in with the highest aspirations
of men. In 1957, the National Council of Churches held a consultation at Haverford College on cooperatives and mutual
business. It was my privilege to be Chairman of this meeting.
The report, the result of the deliberations of fifty men and
women, compiled by Dr. Benson Y. Landis, is a milestone in
cooperative literature. (See Appendix 2.) In 1960, the National

Catholic Rural Life Conference published a special issue on cooperatives,[8] and in 1961 Pope John XXIII promulgated a Papal Encyclical in which he strongly endorsed cooperatives. (See Appendix 3.)

Cooperatives Are Common Denominators in Solving Problems of Freedom

I have had the honor to participate in almost every meeting of the American Institute of Cooperation since 1935, and I believe the following is the most important statement I ever made:

> Cooperatives are as necessary to freedom as rain is to harvest.
>
> Cooperatives can only perform their ultimate service to all mankind when their members recognize that women have brains for far more than merely being pretty and tending the hearthstone—important as are both of these functions. Why cannot men alone do the job? Because they operate on hunches, which are often wrong, and women by intuition, which is more often right.
>
> Cooperatives can become the common denominator in helping to solve the problems inherent in the developing areas. If we do not assume the responsibility gained *here* from our experiences, and help people *there* to help themselves, there is no question about it but that the "compulsory" type state-dominated "cooperatives" behind the iron curtain will take over in other new areas and freedom will be lost to more millions and millions of people.
>
> When cooperatives realize their power, when men and women in policy and decision making positions have learned to work together and with other groups using the nonprofit "corporate person," then cooperatives will become catalysts for freedom in the community of nations.

[8]*See "How Cooperatives Build Rural Life,"* Catholic Rural Life *(Oct., 1960).*

A Conservative Looks At Cooperatives

Farmers produce the food, fiber, and shelter products upon which national and international prosperity is built, and too often receive little in return.[9] Oliver Goldsmith recognized this when he said:

> Ill fares the land, to hast'ning ills a prey,
> Where wealth accumulates, and men decay;
> . . . a bold peasantry, their country's pride,
> When once destroyed, can never be supplied.

By use of the cooperative principle, farm people are trying to rectify this inequity. The economic existence of the villager is perforce dependent upon agricultural revenue.

Something over a generation ago, Congress became cognizant of the danger of the agrarian situation and, together with various state legislatures, passed several enabling Acts allowing farm people to create cooperative corporations to perform for themselves certain specific group services which they did not enjoy individually. It is interesting to note that, in discussions preliminary to the passing of these statutes, it was emphasized time and again that cooperatives promote the national welfare.

Financed Largely by Borrowings from Members

Farmer cooperatives are permitted to raise capital through the sales of stock yielding a statutory limited return to the holders. The dividend rate on the stock or membership capital of cooperative associations is by law restricted to what the legislature considers a fair rate of interest, usually not exceeding 8% or the legal rate of interest in the State. Proprietary corporations, on the other hand, may set whatever dividend rate they wish. The payment of a fair rate of return by cooperatives on their

[9]This material is from "Both Ends of the Track," an address by Raymond W. Miller before New York City Rotary Club, November 29, 1945.

stock or membership capital is regarded generally by members as *an operating expense, like interest paid on borrowed money,* and should not be regarded as an ordinary dividend on stock because members usually furnish all needed capital.

Federal statutes, providing for the exemption of farmer cooperatives meeting prescribed conditions, authorize such cooperatives to accumulate a reasonable amount of reserves. However, neither reserves nor dividends present any significant problem. Most cash reserves of cooperatives consist merely of deferred payments or refunds and are really capital borrowed from their membership. In an increasingly large number of cases, such capital exists as revolving-fund. The Commissioner of Internal Revenue has issued rulings with respect to taxing patronage equities so retained. This whole problem is handled by the Bureau of Internal Revenue, carrying out the will of Congress as expressed in the statute; the intent of the legislation is to give to farm people the opportunity to meet capital requirements, more or less on a parity with those in other lines of business.

Cooperatives Are Private Enterprises; Feature Democratic Control

Farmer cooperatives are private enterprises with democratic control. Farmer cooperatives are a natural business development within a democracy, because they are democratic in form, practice, and principle. They have absorbed the New England town meeting idea in their functioning.

In addition to the economic advantage of cooperative action by farm people, there are intangible, spiritual results. The mere fact that farm families meet on a commodity or business basis to help one another in an economic way promotes increased interest in those virtues that are roughly defined by the term "spiritual." Democracy in government can become more workable when there are groups of people within it using a cooperative method in dealing with one another.

A Conservative Looks At Cooperatives

Cooperatives Foster Upgrading of Diet

The greatest domestic postwar need for all America, rural and urban, is the upgrading of the American diet. The rank and file of the American people do not appreciate the full meaning of these words. This nation cannot stand the high cost of continued malnutrition. A saddeningly large percentage of young men were unfit for military service because of physical defects, many of which were attributable to poor nutrition.

Incidentally, malnutrition is not confined to the homes of the poor. Many nutritionists and home economists are convinced that inadequate diet today is more prevalent among the upper strata of society than the lower. Richly flavored or attractive foods often conceal mineral, vitamin or caloric deficiencies. The food value that the simple farmer gets from a potato skin is often far in excess of high-priced Fifth Avenue fare.

Food questions are of importance to every city dweller. They are also of great interest to the farmer. Alone, he can do little to help city dwellers get better food for their money. But, through his cooperative organization, he can conduct significant research in how to produce better food stuffs. Commercial food handlers should be as much interested in such research as the farmer.

THERMOMETERS OR THERMOSTATS

Are we thermometers or thermostats? The thermometer is a very valuable instrument; however, it simply records the temperature at any given moment.[10] The thermostat, on the other hand, keeps the temperature at a given level. The thermostat instigates action.

We, as individuals, too often choose to become mere thermometers. This is the easy way of life, and those who follow

[10]*This and the following paragraphs are from an address by Raymond W. Miller at the Annual Meeting, Consumers Cooperative Association, Kansas City, Missouri, November, 1961.*

44

it are typified by the remark, "Well, I'm just killing time." "Killing time" is destroying one of the most valuable things in life.

Cooperatives are designed to operate as thermostats. The idea of nonprofit cooperation is that, while making no profit itself, the cooperative, by its actions, enables others to make a profit. Cooperatives were set up to help change the times, with the goal of a better world. They have had an amazing history. In my opinion, cooperatives have been, are, and will continue to operate as thermostats.

However, there is a tendency for cooperatives, as they become larger and more important, to operate only as thermometers. The cooperative movement will die unless this tendency is reversed. In my view the death of the cooperative movement would be disastrous for America as a whole. Cooperatives act as pacesetters for other businesses in ways that will be most beneficial for their members. So they resemble the thermostat; they do not operate as proprietary business does for the sake of profit for a limited few, in that they may be "set" to assure conditions that have been agreed upon as goals.

Important Cooperative Concept of World-Wide Use

Let's consider the tremendous changes which have taken place in farmer cooperatives during the last fifty years. Until the passage of the federal Capper-Volstead law in 1922 and state agricultural cooperative marketing laws of about that year, it was regarded as illegal for farm people to form cooperatives for marketing their produce. Court decisions handed down during the early years of this century indicate that some farmers went to jail for pooling their produce and marketing it collectively. They were accused of breaking the antitrust laws. Then pioneers across this nation began the long, slow process of legal change whereby it became possible for farm people to join together in forming a service organization through which they might market their products. There were no great objections to people purchasing together, either here or in the British Empire. However, the marketing cooperative is definitely a product of Anglo-Saxon law of this century, with most of the legal pioneering being done in the United States and Canada. *This cooperative concept is perhaps the most important thing we export today in our attempt to help raise the world-wide standard of living.*

Farmer cooperatives, both purchasing and marketing, have been responsible for many things besides the actual handling of commodities and supplies. They have given farmers status in the community as respected businessmen. Often a farm represents an investment of $100,000 to $200,000.

Rural America Greatly Benefited by Cooperatives

The farmer cooperative is definitely a "think shop" for efficiency and democracy. Aside from its other values, it is a common meeting place where men and their families are able to take their ideas and, with the help of the Extension Service of the Land Grant Colleges and the United States Department of Agriculture weld them with the ideas of others. High school educators, by means of farmer cooperatives, develop a whole new phase of agricultural and world development. This blending of the thought of farmers, university faculties, and government officials is unique in history. Out of this we are building the new rural America.

The farmer cooperative has also been a roadblock to cartels. Cartels breed communism, for the trust mind is not the true representative of democracy.

Women Are Assets as Cooperative Directors

There have been mistakes made. Some farm leaders have used the Capper-Volstead and other enabling Acts as license to do whatever they pleased. Recently the Supreme Court of the United States, in a unanimous opinion, said that farm people

46

organizing cooperatives are not conspiring in restraint of trade, but that the cooperatives, once formed, must live under the same laws of morality, fair play, justice, and non-exploitation as do other organizations. It is my personal opinion that members of cooperatives ought to recognize that perhaps the best way to create a moral and ethical climate is to put women on their boards of directors. A woman is a natural moralist.

The drive for decent grain sanitation in international markets has come from the farmers. We, in America, at times shortsightedly shipped poor, unclean grain overseas—in many cases losing the markets as a consequence. The farm organizations of North America continue their fight for better grain sanitation standards.

III. Where Cooperatives Are Strong, Communism Cannot Exist

"The battle for the world is between those who believe in cooperation and those who believe in compulsion."

"Freedom is most secure in those countries which use cooperatives as a basic part of their capitalistic economy. Communism, on the other hand, finds a toehold and grows among the population in those areas where cooperatives are either nonexistent or very weak."

"Cooperatives are the seedbeds of democracy."

VOLUNTARY ASSOCIATIONS—HYBRIDIZERS FOR DEMOCRACY

Voluntary association—voluntary organization—benefits people. And voluntary association, in turn, receives the benefit of people—the benefit of people thinking and working together.[1] Voluntary association is the very foundation upon which America's greatness has been built. It is a recognition—and acceptance—of the fact that individual good stems from the general good. More and more, people everywhere are beginning to realize that they will find greater strength and security

[1] *This and the following paragraphs are from an address by Raymond W. Miller at the annual meeting of Producers Seed Company, affiliate of Illinois Agricultural Association, Chicago, Illinois, November 14, 1960. Published in* VITAL SPEECHES *(February 1, 1961), 238. See also George Romney, "The Force of Voluntary Cooperation,"* JOURNAL, *American Society of Association Executives (January 1960).*

in voluntarily associating themselves with others. This is truly the new frontier.

The ages of mankind have developed and tested many ways of life, many social and economic systems, and many systems of government. Plato, for example, brought forward in *The Republic* a concept of the ideal state. But Plato's Republic was, in reality, only a smooth and streamlined framework for a highly *dictatorial form* of government. His Republic was not a voluntary association and hence no Republic at all.

Let me say again: Voluntary association—voluntary organization—benefits people, and receives the benefit of people. Why do I stress this? Because this is the fundamental difference —the dividing line—between the philosophy of the free world and the philosophy of the totalitarian states. Voluntary organizations are people's organizations. But dictators do not like people's organizations; they want to keep people in the dark.

A Practical Way to Launch a Democracy

A practical way to launch democracy in a country is to begin with voluntary organizations, and to build up a multitude of such associations. A country should have farmer groups, credit unions, mutual funds, trade associations, press associations, chambers of commerce, and so on.

When people gather together in small groups to help run their business, they are not only making industry function productively, but they are also developing a better notion of what a democratic system of government actually is—and how it functions.

It Is What We Actually Do That Counts

Voluntary associations in the public interest are one of North America's unique contributions. We don't expect the rest of the world to copy what we have done, but to adapt our procedure to the respective needs of different countries.

50

Use of Cooperative Idea Abroad Becomes Seedbed for Democracy

In my recent book *Can Capitalism Compete?* I made the following comment:

> THE COOPERATIVE, the nonprofit cooperation associa-
> tion, as it is used in North America, is something that
> fascinates overseas leaders, but unfortunately only a few
> coming here under any auspices get acquainted with it.
> Unless the visitors are farmers or actual operators of
> consumer cooperatives, they seldom hear of our cooper-
> atives; or if they do, they are told: "Cooperatives are
> not good for America—they are socialistic." Nothing is
> more capitalistic than a corporation for service without
> entity-profit, but with profit to the members who use and
> own it—such as the Associated Press, Sunkist, Railway
> Express Agency, Land O'Lakes, Equitable Life Assurance
> Society, our credit union finance companies, and agricul-
> tural purchasing associations.
>
> The Scandinavian countries are "loved" in all parts
> of the world largely because of their "middle way." We
> have a similar development here, but we do not talk
> about it enough. B. J. Patel, of India, a businessman
> devoting his life to the betterment of his people, was in
> the United States, and we talked for hours about this
> whole situation. He visited cooperatives in many sections
> of the country, and then at the request of his government
> went to Red China to study their state-dictated "cooper-
> atives." His minority report pointed out that the cooper-
> atives in China are not truly cooperatives, but are really
> economic divisions of the government; that while real
> democratic, capitalistic cooperatives can build men of in-
> dependent thought, will, and initiative, government or-
> ganization destroys all this.[2]

Cooperation in a World of Competition

In my wanderings around the world—some three hundred thousand miles among its trouble spots—I have come

[2]CAN CAPITALISM COMPETE? *(New York, 1949), p. 236.*

to the conclusion that the battle for the world is between those who believe in cooperation and those who believe in compulsion.[3]

KOINONIA is a voluntary association, an experiment in voluntary cooperation, and one of my strongest beliefs is that democratic government cannot last very long without a tremendous number of voluntary organizations to back it up. My observation is that democracy succeeds in direct proportion to the number of voluntary organizations in a country.

In most of the new nations, the people just do not know how to cooperate. They have emerged from a dictatorial form of tribal government and colonialism. A practical way to build the democratic idea into a country—to help them to help themselves—is to start voluntary organizations that will show them how cooperation works.

Today our country is competing for the minds of men. We have chosen to compete *by the method of cooperation*. At the end of World War II, we could have conquered the world. We had the power to do it. But we, as a people, chose rather to cooperate with the world. We have spent billions in trying to follow this path. Some of our money has been unwisely spent. But I think we have given the world the *chance* to cooperate.

The Moslems have a proverb, "To understand a man, you've got to walk a mile in his shoes, whether they fit or not." Walking in another man's shoes isn't easy. An institution with which I am connected has made a long series of studies on how to understand others. Here are a few points from these studies:

- Normal man is subject to rational response, if he is approached with recognition of what he wants.
- Man wants a purpose in life. Give people a purpose. They want recognition. They want participation. Down

[3]*This and the following paragraphs are from an article by Raymond W. Miller in* Koinonia Magazine, *published by the Koinonia Foundation of Baltimore (June 1961), 30.*

underneath, they have concern for people (if it doesn't cost too much).

- And they want something bigger than themselves.
- Man wants an ultimate in life. He wants knowledge. And he wants the right of free discussion. Very few people have it.
- Man responds more readily if we can get him to realize that he *should* do something rather than that he *shall* do it. In the slave world, it's *you shall*.

How does cooperation fit in a world of competition? I wrote a book about it and barely scratched the surface. Perhaps what we really need to know about it is compressed in The Sermon on the Mount. Cooperation, communication, understanding—at bottom the answer is always spiritual. So it is with democracy and the real meaning of America and the dignity of man. At the most meaningful level, these are spiritual matters. We'd better quit preaching Christ unless we mean it. If we merely sound off, we'll fail.

COMMUNISM—CAPITALISM—COOPERATION. DEMOCRACY ITSELF IS A GREAT COOPERATIVE

Here in North America, our economic system has not remained static. We have improved it over what it was a century ago. We have, as a matter of fact, developed an entirely *new kind of capitalism*.[4]

To differentiate our present-day North American capitalism from the monopoly capitalism which Karl Marx saw in his day,

[4]*This and other paragraphs from a presentation by Raymond W. Miller at the 33rd annual meeting of the American Institute of Cooperation, University of Minnesota, Minneapolis, Minnesota, August 23, 1961, published in* VITAL SPEECHES *(October 15, 1961), and* AMERICAN COOPERATION, 1961. *Presented to the U. S. Senate in Speech of Hon. Hubert H. Humphrey of Minnesota and published in* CONGRESSIONAL RECORD *(September 1, 1961).*

our present-day system may be termed *Cooperative-Service Capitalism*. It is the antithesis of communism. Cooperative-Service Capitalism combines the basic principles of participation, self-help, and social concern in the use of capital. Within it, labor, management, and capital form a triumvirate that makes possible a consumer-economy based upon the theory of abundance rather than scarcity. Within it, capitalistic enterprises develop along various lines: profit and loss corporations, nonprofit cooperative corporations, individual enterprises, and partnerships.

Social and economic mobility differentiates this form of capitalism from the strictures and personal restrictions inherent in the state capitalism of modern dictatorial communism. Our new capitalism participates in producing economic progress through social justice by democratic means.

Canada and the United States have developed this same general type of cooperative-service capitalism and have largely put the old exploitative type in legal strait jackets.

The cooperative is a nonprofit corporation organized to serve its members at cost. Its members join voluntarily and may withdraw membership and patronage at will. It is managed by a board of directors elected by the membership, without interference or control by the state. The cooperative offers an opportunity for the "little man" to participate in the benefits of a mass production and distribution economy, and still maintain his individual ownership and identity.

Cooperative-service capitalism has not led to state ownership of all the means of production, as Karl Marx advocated. It has not caused the individual to regress into a mere pawn of the state, as is the case in all of the communist countries today. But it has marvelously succeeded in accomplishing all and more than was valuable in Marx's program.

Our North American system of capitalism centers in the profit motive. It permits the individual citizen to own land and property, productive equipment and resources, to work at a job of his own choosing, to take risks, to compete in the market place—and to keep as his own a fair share of what he earns. But this new capitalism is set up to meet human needs—to create jobs—and to contribute to the general good, as well as to enable employers and employees alike to make money. This system of capitalism recognizes *values in life* above and beyond economic security. It is concerned not only with providing comforts, conveniences, and luxuries for the human body, but it is also concerned with providing for the *betterment of the human spirit.*

Our North American system of capitalism recognizes the worth and dignity of the individual. It encourages initiative and self-reliance. It embodies ethics—although some individuals and corporations, of course, still have ethical lessons to learn.

It is based on man's love of freedom. And it is practical. It works.

Our North American system of service capitalism, as a matter of fact, has proved itself to be by far the best economic system ever devised for producing and distributing an abundance of goods and services for the great mass of the people.

Why Communism Has Gained

Cartels are sires of communism and its resulting slavery because of the frustrations of men and women against the exploitations, abuses, and iron shackles of exploitative capitalism. Communism is largely winning by default, because of the neglect on the part of those "who have," to have compassion for those who "have not."

Cooperatives, an the other hand, are sires of democracy and of freedom, because cooperatives give men and women the opportunity to learn by doing, to participate in their own destiny, both economic and social, and to feel that they belong.

Communism has gained ground largely because the capitalistic free world has failed to explain—and to prove—to the people of the world that *capitalism* has made the gospel of Marx as obsolete as the old belief that the world is flat.

Capitalism can be explained only by capitalists who are

true believers. And cooperatives, being among the most capitalistic of all sectors of twentieth-century capitalism, have neglected to carry the torch of conviction in the crusade for freedom.

Communism is a giant cartel of state capitalism—with men as pawns on the chessboard—and with dictators making the moves. Pawns are always expendable.

Cartelized communism or cooperative-service capitalism— one or the other will be the "wave of the future." Our children's destiny is in our hands. If capitalism is to win in competition with communism, the victory will come only as the result of the determination and efforts of the voluntary apostles and disciples of cooperative-service capitalism who believe in our economic system and our way of life.

Voluntary cooperation is an idea which we can export to the people of the newly developing countries—but not by sitting on our hands—and not by concentrating on our own selfish interests—while the communists are out selling their wares, and often establishing organizations falsely called "cooperatives," which are in fact state institutions and not voluntary organizations of free people.[5]

The Militia of Freedom

In our type of government, the citizens of the land are the militia of freedom. From the War for Independence through the several major wars since, our military has been largely composed of non-professional fighters. When the call of alarm has sounded, the ablebodied men have risen to assume their tasks in line with their abilities.

Today we are engaged in a war of much greater magnitude than any war we have ever known in the past—a cold war for the loyalties of people. In this world-wide engagement, new types of resources are needed. While the military holds the lines

[5]*See, for example, Irving Peter Pflaum,* Tragic Island: How Communism Came to Cuba *(New York, 1961), Chap. 12.*

against a hot, shooting war, the citizens of our nation must rise up and help win the war of ideas.

Each segment of our population has its appointed task: the educator, for instance, to battle in the classroom and the forum for the principles of freedom; the lawyer for world peace through law; the trade union proponent for freedom of choice in working; the economist for social mobility; and so on through a long list of groups who can help build the battlements for liberty.

Dr. Joseph G. Knapp, Administrator of the Farmer Cooperative Service of the U.S.D.A., in the "Report of the Social Science Research Council," said, "The compilation of information is perhaps less important than ability to make good use of it."[6] No truer words were ever uttered concerning the basic cause of the loss of much of the free world to dictators and to slavery.

Cooperatives Have Not Made Good Use of Their Information

The "little people of the world" can understand the message of cooperation and can adapt it to their use in developing a standard of living beyond that offered at the end of the rainbow by the dictators of the Kremlin or Peking. And yet, for a third of a century, during which time communism has grown like the beanstalk in the famous folk story, the American Institute of Cooperation has compiled information and has created the world's greatest library of cooperative literature. But it has done practically nothing more than assemble information and occasionally use it for itself. *It has not taken up the cause of cooperation*—and it has failed to make good use of its information in "saving the world."

[6]*in John D. Black, ed.,* RESEARCH IN AGRICULTURAL COOPERATION *(Social Science Research Council, New York, 1933), p. 27.*

A Conservative Looks At Cooperatives

People can understand the meaning of working together toward a better economic and social existence—in fact, *Communism is not true cooperation but a heresy*.

Where true cooperatives are strong, communism is weak— for example, in Sweden, Switzerland, Norway, the United Kingdom, Denmark, Ireland, Greece, Canada, and the United States. But communism is in a virulent stage in countries where cooperatives are largely unknown, as in some Latin American countries.[7]

The only short-cut to *understanding economic freedom* is through the use of the nonprofit voluntary association. We have spent untold millions with the best of intentions in the newly formed nations, and have had it go down the rat hole, largely because we have not seriously attempted to help the people there understand how to use the cooperative vehicle to carry them over the rough spots.

Japan today is in the camp of the free world, principally because during the MacArthur regime the rural people were encouraged to form agricultural, credit, and fishery cooperatives.

The only setback that communism has received in Italy has been in a section of the country where an American cooperative group took the initiative in helping the people get cooperative credit for their local cooperatives. Murray Lincoln, then President of CARE, helped organize the American group.

Cooperatives Can Be Logical Contacts with the World

Only an infinitesimal part of our overseas development efforts, public and private, has been directed toward teaching people how to found self-help organizations. Most of the failures of our foreign aid program can be attributed to the fact that we have taken the easy path—too much of our overseas time and

[7]*See* AMERICAS *(August 1961), Pan American Union, Washington, D. C.*

58

money has been spent to help governments to do the job when we, at home, know that that is not the way to help the growth of democracy.

American cooperatives are the logical groups to explain how people's organizations disseminate democracy. Invaluable help can be received from the Farmer Cooperative Service and the Small Business Administration of the U.S. Government, but the lead in "showing the world" the fundamental principles of our cooperative organizations must be taken by the voluntary organizations themselves.

The government, of course, must carry out some big enterprises, such as our own Hoover Dam, TVA, and St. Lawrence Development program, but in much of the world we have encouraged the state to go into the areas where a cooperative could not only do the job much better but also be a seminar for democracy. For instance, we have encouraged government to distribute power in new countries but have only since 1962 encouraged use of the REA cooperative principle.

Cooperatives Have Stood Idly by Instead of Taking Initiative

The North Sea Kingdoms have proven that cooperatives are the antithesis of statism and dictatorial communism and, at the same time, do not eliminate ordinary profit-and-loss private business. The amazing thing is that as cooperatives have served and flourished in these countries and on our continent, ordinary enterpreneur enterprises have likewise prospered. The nonprofit cooperative not only helps in its selected field, but acts as a stimulus and guide for other business.

Most of the world thinks that it must choose either the cartel or communism. But there is a third little understood alternative: the cooperative.

Unless the "little people" of the world can learn to use the nonprofit device of a self-help cooperative for certain of their needs, communism will sweep the world. Those of us in the

59

free world who have learned to build self-help devices have an obligation to let the world know how such devices are created and operated.

Summary of Ideas on Communism—Capitalism—Cooperatives

I should like to give in condensed form a few of the ideas presented so far.

Cooperatives prove that great people are ordinary people captured by a great idea.

There are a half million words in the English language and the one that has the highest motivation index is *participation*.

There is no human satisfaction equal to that which comes of doing work that is *creative*.

Emotion often obscures problems.

This is the age of revolution—will it bring us freedom or slavery?

Cooperative effort trains men to combine enthusiasm with humility; the word *we* becomes all-important, rather than *I*.

The day-by-day difference between the Soviet philosophy and the cooperative philosophy is this: In the Sino-Soviet world, the organization is more important than the people; in democracies, people are more important than the organization.

Democracy itself is a great cooperative.

Cooperation is not only a good economic device, but a teacher in the school of freedom.

Co-ops Must Assume Rightful Leadership Position

I recommend that our cooperatives assume their rightful position of responsible leadership, by appointing an across-the-board commission of agricultural, credit union, consumer, and service cooperative technicians who, without delay, will make available to the world the fundamental principles of self-help.

Remember, we *are* mobilizing in a total war of ideas.

This will take time, energy, and money—but of what value are these, if the rainbow of freedom vanishes from mankind?

This is *today*. This is our day. Yesterday is but a cancelled check, and tomorrow is a promissory note. But today is cash. Our place in history is right now.

Time is of the essence. Shakespeare in *Julius Caesar* well expressed centuries ago the mandate for those who believe in Cooperative Capitalism when he said:

> There is a tide in the affairs of men,
> Which, taken at the flood, leads on to fortune;
> Omitted, all the voyage of their life
> Is bound in shallows and in miseries.
> On such a full sea are we now afloat;
> And we must take the current when it serves,
> Or lose our ventures.

What Can Cooperatives Do to Sustain Their Part in the Free World?

One of the things I have learned is that as people emerge from illiteracy they want to participate. I should like to make clear, however, that nothing that I say here should be construed as an attack against business as a whole. I like business. I am delighted that there are such things as great profit businesses. I teach in the Harvard Business School, which is sometimes spoken of as the "West Point" of capitalism. It probably is, but the fact remains that a big or a medium-sized profit business cannot be understood by the ordinary person. He cannot participate in it. That is one of the reasons why communism appeals to many groups. It promises people participation[8]

I was in the Philippines with the Hukbalahaps, who were

[8]*This and other paragraphs from "What Can Cooperatives Do to Sustain Their Part in the Free World?" an address by Raymond W. Miller, at the 1962 Farmers Grain Dealers Association Meeting, Fort Des Moines Hotel, Des Moines, Iowa, January 24, 1962.*

revolutionaries. Except for a few leaders, the great bulk of the Huks were just farmers tired of being poor. They wanted to participate in their economy.

Cooperatives—the Answer to Communism

A cooperative is a group of people with a common need who have banded themselves together to do many things they are unable to do as individuals. There, frankly, is the philosophy back of the greatest single answer to communism in the world today. Basically the philosophy is "Does a man participate and still keep his freedom? Does he have a right to join or not join?" You might say, "Fine, that's good, but what does that mean to me?" I have some grandchildren. Lots of people have grand-children, and lots have children. There is more than an even chance that some mother who is now thirty or forty, before she dies, will take her little girl or little grandchild and quietly and while nobody is listening try to explain to that child "Mary, when I was a little girl we had freedom," and that little girl won't know what she is talking about.

Now, don't think that's overdrawn; it's not. People from Korea can say it is true of North Korea. People who have visited East Germany know it's true. I talked with two women I know who escaped recently from Mesopotamia. One of them, a brilliant Lutheran woman, the wife of a pastor, told me how she took her little grandchild, eight years old, in her arms and whispered to her "When I was a girl we had liberty," and that little child didn't know what she was talking about.

Today communism is growing rapidly. The noose is getting tighter around our neck every day. Whether communism wins or not is up to us.

As a lawyer I will start by giving a little bit of evidence. While I don't know all the world I have plenty of friends who do. On the basis of what I have been told I can say that *I know of no place in the world today where communism has grown at all where cooperatives were strong.*

Cooperatives Help Build Stable Japan

In 1944, John Cooper, of the St. Paul Bank for Cooperatives, was sent for by General MacArthur. What was he asked to do? To carry a gun and shoot somebody? No, he was asked to make a study prior to the invasion.

John Cooper didn't go to Japan until the day after the invasion. He landed there with no gun. He landed behind the troops. What did he do? He went across Japan and sold the Japanese the philosophy of our cooperatives.

My friend Murray D. Lincoln, president of the Nationwide Insurance Company, which used to be Ohio Farm Bureau Insurance Company, got so excited over what was going on that he authorized me to go and see what was happening.[9] There were 35,000 rural cooperatives organized in Japan within four years. Japan today is stable and on the side of the free world. Why? Because 35,000 cooperatives were the hybridzers for representative democracy.

Can Democracy Be Strong Without Cooperatives?

There are areas in Europe drifting towards communism. These are areas where cooperatives are weak. I repeat again: *I know of no place in the free world or any place in the world where democracy is strong unless cooperatives are strong.* I know of no place where communism is strong that has voluntary cooperatives. We have the answer, not the only answer, but we have a basic answer; and if we want to get into Christian doctrine, it may go back to the teachings of Jesus who taught the philosophy of man's relationship to man. It is the gospel of Christ, or the Code of Christ, as opposed to the Code of Marx.

So the cooperative movement is important. Now, a person might say, "What can I do to help?" He can say truthfully, "I never saw a communist under my bed." Of course he hasn't,

[9]*See also Murray D. Lincoln,* Vice President in Charge of Revolution *(New York, 1960), pp. 249-257.*

and he probably never will. However, each man has his sphere of influence. The time has come for all of us to study impartially and learn about cooperatives.

Cooperatives Must Take Greater Interest in World Problems

How did the idea for the Common Market come into existence? In 1951, I was in Germany at a meeting of the Ecumenical Conference on European Unity. What was it for? To create public opinion out of which would come a common market and a common organization in order to block the inroads of the materialistic atheism of the U.S.S.R. It was the birth of what we now call the Common Market.

Study the Common Market. Know what is going on. We should spend a lot of time observing such developments not only for the sake of our own chickens, corn and wheat, but also because of their effect upon the world in general.

Let us also take a look at the fragmentation of nations in the world—particularly in Africa where there are approximately thirty countries. These countries would seem unlikely to be successful. We were taught in our schools that America became strong because the thirteen original colonies united. We have been cooperatively-minded from the beginning. It is time that we helped the new countries understand the value of cooperation. If we do not we will see the creation of a power vacuum in Africa.

We must become more conscious of the non-European peoples. Members of North American cooperatives have not been aware enough that people of the other races have intelligence. I have attended cooperative meetings across America for thirty years. I have seldom seen a non-Caucasian member of the cooperative elevated to an official position of importance. We had better begin to take a look and realize that intelligence has nothing to do with color or place of birth.

64

One of the biggest criticisms of us abroad is that practically all the men we send to teach the theory of cooperatives have a European ancestry. Fortunately, this situation has improved in recent years. For example, the Cooperative League selected as director of its operations in India a young American Negro, Dr. Allie Felder. Dr. Felder is a graduate of Hampton Institute, has a Master's degree from the University of Illinois, and a doctorate from Ohio State University. He not only represents the Cooperative League well, according to Wallace J. Campbell, a member of the Nationwide Cooperative Study Team which recently completed a mission to India, but "is highly respected by everyone in the cooperative movement and the highest ranking officials in the Government of India. The fact he is colored and carries his responsibilities so naturally, is a living rebuttal of all the arguments the communists have used in what they call 'American racism' with the people in Southeast Asia."

Women Should Be Recognized for Executive Ability

Our cooperatives must learn the hard way, as people in Asia and Japan have learned, that the brains of women must be recognized. Go to any meeting of scientists or diplomats or executives, representatives of the Iron Curtain countries. Many of those attending are women. They are not there because they are secretaries or concubines but because they have "brains." The scientific world today is shocked by the growth of science behind the Iron Curtain and the Bamboo Curtain. Why? One of the reasons the Iron Curtain countries are ahead of us is because they are capitalizing on the brainpower of women.

A friend of mine, a Canadian scientist, recently visited a great scientific installation in China. While there, he learned that of 4,000 people receiving advanced degrees in science one out of every three is a woman. Cooperatives have been slow to use women's talents. I was delighted when I was in Milwaukee and I found that the assistant director of a large cooperative there is a woman. She is doing a great job.

A Conservative Looks At Cooperatives

Cooperation and the Struggle to Save Capitalism

Cooperatives are the custodians of the most successful vaccine that has yet been discovered to immunize against Communism. And we sit complacently with our hands in our pockets; we "wait for George to do it."[10]

Cooperators Don't Peddle Their Wares

The government of the United States and the government of our friendly crown democracy to the north, Canada, have gone farther in trying to make it possible for people throughout the world to understand cooperatives than have the members of cooperatives themselves. Very few cooperators seem to be giving any thought at all to the fact that this voluntary association of free people operating within the orbit of a capitalistic society is something the world wants.

The Threat Is Dictatorship

Let's take a look at the people in the world for whose good will we are striving. Communism is trying to get them on its side, not by the nondictatorial communism of the New Testament, but by dictatorial means. We are not up against "communism." We are up against *dictatorship* which has adopted the word "communism" as its name. My own opinion is that most of the real communists were shot a long time ago. The Kremlin and Peking use the word communism but are actually slave states.

The Appeal of Communism—Pseudoparticipation

What do the communists do? They go to people and tell them, now you become a part of the communist world; you can *participate*. And my guess is that they do participate, pro-

[10]*This and other paragraphs from an address by Raymond W. Miller at the Kentucky Agricultural Cooperative Conference, University of Kentucky, February 19-20, 1962.*

vided they keep within the restrictions. You can participate in a jail. They offer people that kind of participation. Individually, half the people of the earth don't own as much as the value of our clothes. We can't get such people excited about abstractions like capitalism and private enterprise.

Christian Missionaries Awakened the Poor to the Vision of Something Better

The poverty-stricken peoples have awakened suddenly from their sleep. What awakened them? The Christian missionaries we sent from America and Europe. Few accepted Christ as a Savior, but the vision of something better than they had swept across large areas. The first man who made me aware of what the gospel has meant to the underprivileged peoples was Mr. Nehru. He said, "You know, Mr. Miller, this revolution started with the Christian missionaries."

In North America, we developed a system of political co-operation. It is not perfect; but it allowed the little man, who owned only the shirt on his back and a few tools, to cooperate with other little men and do big things.

Cooperatives Offer Hope of Realizing the Dream

There is a cooperative four miles out of the city of Calcutta, an area inhabited by the poorest of the poor! In 1949, a high caste Brahman Hindu "got the vision" of something better from a Rotary Club in America. This one Hindu went into a fishing community. He helped the low caste organize a cooperative. Take my word for it, the total wealth of the whole community did not exceed $16 per person. That's all there was in 1949. By good fortune, I met the leader of the cooperative, and since that time have kept informed of the cooperative's progress.

What have these fishermen done? They rented five rooms in nearby Calcutta and converted them into a hospital. They have built a school house. Three bright boys and three bright girls from this community are chosen each year to go to the University. They are supported by the community through their cooperative. The community also hired two teachers, who are teaching both adults and children. Now in this community 75 percent are literate, while in 1949 not over 8 percent were literate. Juvenile delinquency is gone.

Let's look at Hong Kong. In 1949, I had the rare opportunity of being in the New Territories in Hong Kong. There I sat on the side of a truck with a Roman Catholic priest, watching a little cooperative community doing some work.

It so happens that this was also the day when the Red Army moved in across the field. I didn't realize I was watching history, but just over the border I saw Chinese boys put up their little pill boxes and bring in their machine guns. They were nice, clean-looking Chinese, even in their ragged uniforms. In the New Territories of Hong Kong about 50,000 Chinese farmers farm right alongside the border. There's an electrified fence there now, with communism on one side and freedom on the other. Since the war, largely as the result of the work of a Quaker gentleman from Britain and a Roman Catholic boy, these Chinamen have learned to help themselves to economic freedom. I'd say practically all of them belong to cooperatives.

Those farmers are participating in our new world. We have the answer, but we're not doing very much about it. We're still too apathetic.

Let's Raise Our Sights

Let's raise our sights; let's think big! We want freedom, but remember, communism is still on the move. It's moving rapidly. The only possible way for us to get ahead of communism in these underdeveloped territories is to give the people something in which they can participate. We don't make fighters for freedom when we give charity handouts.

Out from Oklahoma in 1950 there came a man, Henry Bennett, President of Oklahoma A. & M. Henry Bennett had a dream; he had a vision that the world could be made better by teaching the doctrine of self-help in underdeveloped areas. As head of Point 4, the technical assistance program of the U.S. government, he had the world for his parish, but he was killed in line of duty in a plane crash near Teheran. There haven't been enough people to pick up the mantle that fell when Henry Bennett died.

Congress has attempted to save the world by big gifts. It doesn't work. People with children know that overindulgence is the quickest way to spoil a child. But if you help a child to build something for himself, then you've helped him to be a better adult. In the same way cooperatives help the little people to build a better world for themselves.

The World Is Ready for Our Message

A few years ago, through the inspiration of Murray Lincoln and the backing of his associates, some "crusaders" went to Italy and set up a bank for cooperatives. The operation has been profitable. In the last election, the communists showed a heavy decline in those areas where banks to finance cooperatives had been organized. Other similar but no less dramatic examples could be cited from other parts of the world.

Cooperatives don't have to take over the whole world; there is room for all types of capitalistic business. I know of no cooperative leader who has any reputation who accepts the idea that the whole world ought to be a cooperative commonwealth. Capitalism is at its best when people participate in all types of capitalistic organizations.

IV. Cooperatives In North America

"The nonprofit corporation falls into various categories from giant insurance companies, commonly spoken of as mutuals, to small associations of individual taxicab owners with a dozen members. These mutual or cooperative corporations all have one thing in common—to perform a service for their members at cost."

"Cooperatives are a part of our enlightened twentieth-century Service Capitalism. I believe that 90 percent or more of all Americans are part of one or more cooperatives. I believe that within their structure lies a legal device that the rest of the world can and will increasingly use. This nonprofit segment of the capitalistic field has no quarrel with the profit section. In some areas the one is more appropriate, and in other areas the other—but they both are capitalistic."

THE NONPROFIT CORPORATION

The corporation, dating back to at least 2200 B.C., is an invisible "person" existing only in contemplation of the law.[1] However, it is only within the past one hundred years that the limited liability corporation has begun to assume a major place in business. The corporation is, in a broad sense, both a public and a private "servant" that can be used for the purpose for which it has been chartered by the state. It is formed at the request of certain natural persons and becomes an inanimate person to do their bidding within the legal limitations prescribed

[1]THE STANDARD DICTIONARY OF FACTS *(Buffalo, New York, 1922), pp. 55-7. See also W.P.J. O'Meara, K.C.,* CANADA CORPORATION MANUAL *(Toronto, Canada, 1949), p. 503.*

by the state which charters it.[2]

Most Corporations Are Formed for Profit; Some Are Non-profit

Corporations function in many areas of activity. There are those that are formed purely for charitable purposes and are commonly spoken of as eleemosynary corporations. There are educational corporations which are chartered to offer educational opportunities, such as colleges or universities, music schools, etc. Most of these are nonprofit. However, there are many educational corporations that do operate for profit, particularly in the technical and vocational fields of learning.

The corporation that is of the widest use is, of course, the profit business corporation, chartered by the state and allowed to issue stock as an investment to interested parties and to enter into business arrangements with third parties for the economic benefit of its first party member stock owners. The state is the invisible second party, having the function of protecting the public interest. It has the power to modify or revoke the charter of the business corporation if it does not perform as its charter prescribes or as the legislature may later determine it shall act in the public interest. If the company acts beyond its charter, the act is commonly spoken of as "ultra vires."[3]

Nonprofit Corporation Has Single Objective: To Serve Its Members at Cost

The business corporation not for profit falls into various categories ranging from giant insurance companies, commonly

[2]*Orie L. Phillips and A. Sherman Christenson, "Should Corporations Be Regarded as Citizens within the Diversity Jurisdiction Provisions?"* AMERICAN BAR ASSOCIATION JOURNAL, *XLVIII (May 1962), 435.*
[3]*See H. E. Erdman, "The Associated Dairies of New York as Precursors of American Agricultural Cooperatives," reprinted from* AGRICULTURAL HISTORY, *XXXVI, No. 2 (1962), 82-90.*

spoken of as mutuals, to small associations of individual taxicab owners with a dozen members. These mutual or cooperative corporations all have one thing in common—to perform a service for their members at cost. If the cooperative should make a profit from nonmembers, then this profit automatically puts the company in the category of being in part a profit and loss corporation, subject to the corporate income tax on any earnings on nonmember business.

There has been no real catalogue made, nor could there readily be, of the number of actual types of business performed by nonprofit corporations. It is reasonably certain that neither the profit-entity corporation nor the nonprofit business corporation can wholly preempt the field because they are formed for such different purposes—in one case to make a profit from non-stockholder customers, in another case not to make a profit but to serve members and nonmember patrons at cost.

Those who elect to form a corporation designed to make a profit automatically create a tax gatherer for the government, not a taxpayer, because the income taxes paid by a corporation are really furnished by others.[4] The corporation merely collects

[4]*The corporation income tax is borne by individuals, either in their capacity as consumers to the extent that it is shifted forward or in their capacity as stockholders to the extent that it is not shifted forward. The extent to which it is shifted forward is a matter of much debate, but in any case the corporation income tax is capricious in its impact on individuals. It can take no account of the differing economic positions of stockholders. Nor can it take any account of differences in the economic circumstances of individuals who purchase the products of corporations. And not the least of the disadvantages of the corporation income tax is that it appears to be a painless method of financing government expenditures simply because it is not easily visible to the individual. Its use fosters the illusion that nobody pays. Foregoing taken from "Federal Tax Issues in 1955," a Statement on National Policy by the Research and Policy Committee of the Committee for Economic Development (New York, May, 1955).*

73

taxes from customers or stockholders (depending upon whether the burden is shifted forward or not) and holds them in trust until paid to the government.

People Have Freedom to Choose Type of Corporation Desired

If the people organizing a company do not wish to pay a corporate income tax, they can easily form a corporation that by its very charter denies it the right to make a profit; and a great many companies operate on this basis, particularly in the fields of agricultural marketing and supply. People who promote nonprofit business or finance corporations such as credit unions are primarily interested in effecting savings by an economic service at cost. They are not ordinarily seeking stock bonuses from capital growth nor returns on capital above what building and loan companies would pay on investments. It is purely a matter of which type of corporation the stockholders desire to have the state charter.

It is also interesting to note that many profit and loss corporations, in order to hold their own in the heavy competition with larger corporations, will often jointly form a nonprofit organization that will purchase or perform other services for them on a cost basis.

Many Types of Organizations Performing Nonprofit Services for Members

There are many fields in which the nonprofit business corporation has become established and is performing a valuable economic service. The following list is not intended to be all-inclusive; it merely points to many types of organizations that are now performing a nonprofit service to their member patrons:

Cemetery associations
Mutual insurance companies:
   life, fire, automobile,
   casualty, etc.

Taxicab associations
Apartment house cooperatives
Trucking associations
Lumberyards

Purchasing associations of many kinds
Research organizations
Mutual investment trusts
Golf and country clubs
Travel clubs
Automobile associations
Credit unions (Probably from the point of view of membership the largest type of nonprofit organization in the business field)
Chambers of Commerce
Florists telegraphic services
Rural electric associations
Farmers' marketing associations
Consumer cooperative stores
Railway terminals
Independent grocery stores (purchasing and operating services)
An airline owned by employees
Publishing companies
Grain terminals
Express companies
Tourist houses
Banks (chartered as mutuals or in some areas as cooperatives)
Geographic societies
College and university student housing (commonly called co-ops)
Radio and television stations
Mutual water districts
Group health associations
Professional associations
Nursery schools
Community playgrounds
Motor Court associations
Vocational Rehabilitation Groups

All of the above and many others are a part of the service capitalistic economy wherein citizens are allowed freedom to choose the corporate structure which best fits their purposes. Nonprofit business corporations operate in direct competition with each other and with either profit and loss business organizations or forms of business which occurs when a government takes over a business and operates it without the cost of a return on capital invested. The major part of all the life insurance written in America is written by mutual or cooperative companies.

Electrical Field Is Example of Three Forms of Enterprise

Examples of these three forms of enterprises—those for profit, those for mutual use at cost, and those owned by a government—are found in the local electric distribution field.

Most of the power distributed from wires in the United States comes from systems that are owned by investors of capital. These systems perform a very creditable service.

However, there are something over 2,000 cities and towns that have determined by vote of their citizens that they want the local government to own the system with its distributing lines. This automatically makes the system a nontaxable government

75

monopoly, sometimes referred to as "creeping socialism."

The third alternative has been used in an increasing number of rural areas where there was no power available. The farmers, together with other ruralists, have organized nonprofit cooperatives that borrowed money from the Rural Electrification Administration of the United States Government and/or private lending agencies to form what are commonly known as Rural Electric Cooperatives. These groups pay property and franchise taxes as do the profit and loss corporations. They are not taken off the tax rolls. They perform a service to their members at cost, but do not ordinarily receive special tax concessions. Some state laws and state constitutional provisions initially allowed REA Cooperatives special rates.[5] The cooperatives have

[5]*These enactments were made in the interest of general welfare and in the hope of stimulating rapid social and economic upgrading in the rural area. These laws and provisions are being eliminated as the rural areas have developed. Many had stipulated terminal dates similar to those given by many areas in the form of tax concessions for new business. An example of this type of legislation is an amendment to Paragraph 2, Section 2, Article 7 of the Constitution of Georgia, approved March 8, 1941. It reads:*

> *There is hereby exempted from all taxation, state, county, municipal, school district, and political or territorial subdivision of the state having the authority to levy taxes, all co-operative, nonprofit, membership corporations organized under the laws of this state for the purpose of engaging in rural electrification, AS DEFINED IN SUB-SECTION 1 OF SECTION 3 OF THE ACT APPROVED MARCH 30, 1937 PROVIDING FOR THEIR INCORPORATION, and all of the real and personal property owned or held by such corporations for such purposes. The exemption herein provided for shall expire twenty years from January 1, 1942.*

> *In accordance with this legislation, on January 1, 1962, the Rural Electric Cooperatives in the State of Georgia are subject to all taxes levied upon their particular form of business and/ or property. Had these electric facilities been built by a state*

borrowed money from the government at a rate of interest fixed by the Congress but this has been and is being paid back on time or ahead of time. The record of payments of these cooperatives to the United States Government is one of the enviable records in the whole financial history of government lending to organizations, either for profit or not for profit.

The Rural Electrification Act of 1936, as amended, (7 U. S. Code 901-24) authorizes the Administrator to make loans for rural electrification to persons, corporations, States, municipalities, other public agencies and to nonprofit associations organized under the laws of the states. The Administrator is also authorized to make loans to establish and to improve and expand rural telephone service.

Although preference is given to public agencies and nonprofit associations for electrification, loans have been made to 24 private power companies. Of 820 loans to improve rural telephone service, 602 had been made to commercial companies as of December, 1963.

Many critics of REA fail to recognize that the Adminis-

or municipal body, they would, in all probability, be removed forever from the tax rolls. As it is, they have received inducement to build in line with many business organizations that are granted temporary tax relief in order to encourage construction.

The late Dr. E. A. Stokdyk, one of the twentieth-century's "greatest searchers for truth" in the economic field, gave great importance to the need for cooperatives to stand on their own financial feet as soon as possible and not be adult toddlers.

The history of the transformation of the units within the United States Farm Credit System from dependence upon federal capital to holding their own in the market-place for money and financing themselves through the sale of debentures to the general public, is one of the most dramatic stories in the whole field of cooperative effort, here or abroad. For further study in this field I recommend Joseph G. Knapp, STOKDYK—ARCHITECT OF COOPERATION (Washington, D. C., 1953), Chap. XI.

trator is authorized to lend money at the statutory rate to cooperatives and noncooperatives alike for rural electric and telephone facilities.

Cooperatives Born of Necessity; Provide Services Not Otherwise Available

As long as people have freedom to organize in a free economy, as they wish, various types of business organizations—those for profit and those not for profit—will continue to exist and compete with each other for recognition. Cooperatives are born of necessity when other forms of business do not provide adequate service at reasonable cost.

Business—profit and loss and nonprofit, together—is the bulwark of the free world against the inroads of statism. However, business itself is to blame for the trend toward government ownership. The people do not rush into state ownership and operation. This development comes only when business has been negligent in providing service at reasonable cost.

Cooperative Farming Questionable

Cooperative farming is unique in that it is the one form of cooperative effort that I have never seen succeed. There may have been efforts that prospered, but I have never seen them, unless one considers the Kibbutz in Israel a cooperative.[6] But they are communal, along the lines of the many efforts of similar nature that have been tried and that have failed in other parts of the world.

They have succeeded in Israel because of a combination of factors: religion, culture, and the drive for a new national homeland. The Kibbutz is being surpassed in Israel, however, by another form of cooperative wherein the ownership of the

[6]See THE COMMONWEALTH, XXXVIII, No. 25 (June 18, 1962), 158, published by The Commonwealth Club, San Francisco, California.

land is vested in the individual farmer. He owns his own home and his basic equipment, but is served by service-type cooperatives.

Cooperatives succeed when they furnish services to the farmer that he cannot individually provide save at excessive cost and effort. Cooperatives fail when they take over the function of the agricultural producer as an individual operator and inevitably stifle initiative and incentive. Cooperatives are a crutch for him to use, but he still must walk by himself.

Man and the soil have an affinity that breeds freedom. When the soil is owned by the group, many sociological and human relations factors mitigate and ruin the effort. Cooperatives are the best guarantee for economic success of the "little lander," for they give him a partnership in the market place. But they are not designed to take the place of individual ownership of the farm. *World Agriculture,* the official publication of the International Federation of Agricultural Producers, 1 Rue d'Hauteville, Paris X, France, for April, 1962, carries a review of two articles published in India by Professors Desai and R. S. Mehta concerning cooperative farming. The concluding paragraphs of the review reveal a deep comprehension of the matter of cooperative farming:

> Co-operation has met with some success in most countries of the world in spheres other than production. But the co-operative method of production, even in spheres other than agriculture, has not achieved significant success anywhere in the world and especially in agriculture with the possible exception of a few countries like Israel. For the success of co-operatives, in general, the membership of the society must be homogeneous in character. But co-operative farming in a village composed of people with divergent viewpoints, ideologies, castes, and other differences becomes difficult of adoption.
>
> The record of the existing co-operative farming societies is not very encouraging. Sathianathan and Ryan from their study of the land colonization societies, concluded that "although the ideals of joint cultivation, joint

harvesting, and profit-sharing have been recommended to the colonist, nowhere has it yet found favour. Each colonist prefers to cultivate his land on his own account and keep to himself the fruit thereof."

It is clear from what has been said above that even in the case of land colonization societies, where lands are given to the society by government, the members have shown an inclination to individual ownership and cultivation. This clearly sets a limit to the organization of co-operative farming societies on ownership holdings. Renewed emphasis should be placed on better organizing and management of the existing co-operative farming societies. Success in these farming societies as demonstrated by better farming, better business, and better living will act as a powerful motivation for farmers to organize new societies.

The long and vigorous debate in India has led to a great new emphasis on service-type cooperatives in agriculture—marketing, purchasing, and credit. There is a diminishing interest in "collective farming," particularly since the failure of the collectives in Red China.

Voluntary Noncommercial Associations Also Part of Cooperative Area

Although this book is primarily devoted to the voluntary membership, nonprofit business organization, its findings are also applicable to the nonprofit trade, cultural, or professional association. There are thousands of voluntary, nonprofit, noncommercial associations in this country. The local chamber of commerce is an example, and other examples include such well known organizations as the National Geographic Society, the American Automobile Association, and the United Business Schools Association. These groups make a significant contribution to our system of free enterprise, and, in fact, help to preserve our liberties.

Basically the same rules of law and procedure apply to noncommercial as to commercial ones: both must conform to the antitrust statutes; both must serve their membership at a reasonable cost.

Cooperatives—Enlightened Capitalism

"Search for truth is the noblest occupation of man—its publication, a duty." So wrote Madame de Stael, the French authoress and foe of the Bonapartes.[7]

Man is the only recording being on this planet. The beasts of the field, the birds of the air, and the fish of the deep all learn by experience—and through millenia of time their accumulated knowledge evolves into hereditary traits which we call "intuition." Man, also intuitive, possesses, in addition, the ability to preserve and transmit his experiences consciously to posterity.

The American Institute of Cooperation is the most significant medium yet created for preserving what men have thought and said about cooperatives. Indeed, the most prized set of books in my personal library is the published record of the annual Institute, the first volume of which was published in 1925. Charles W. Holman, E. G. Nourse, and Richard Pattee comprised the Editorial Board of Volume One; their Foreword reads as follows:

> These volumes contain all of the papers and reports of selected conferences and discussions of the First Summer Session of the American Institute of Cooperation, held at the University of Pennsylvania, July 20-August 15, 1925. In offering them to the public the Trustees believe that they comprise a most valuable collection of information regarding the progress, legal basis, present status and problems of the cooperative movement among the farmers of the United States. In making them avail-

[7]*This and other paragraphs from a presentation by Raymond W. Miller at the summer conference, American Institute of Cooperation, August 9-12, 1959, University of Illinois, Urbana, Illinois, published in* American Cooperation, *1959.*

able in printed form, the Trustees disclaim any responsibility for any of the views expressed. To do so would be to frustrate the purposes of the Institute which, among its other services, is an open forum for the discussion of real cooperative problems.

With this broad concept as a base, succeeding program committees have made it possible for the Institute to become an arsenal of facts, available for universal use as man strives to balance political and economic freedoms.

Examples Cited of Use of Cooperative Idea

Because so many of my overseas friends have asked about the extent of cooperatives and mutual businesses in our American capitalistic economy, I have taken my wife and myself as an example of how an average middle-income couple can be helped by these organizations. At the present time we are members of and utilize the services of the following:

Diamond Walnut Growers: As California walnut producers we, together with several thousand fellow members, cooperatively grade, advertise, and market our crops. We grow our product some 2,500 miles from our average customer. Unless we pooled our off-farm efforts with our fellow growers, we would have no voice in our relationship with the ultimate consumer. Is this socialistic?

National Geographic Society: Together with several million other Americans we, as members, participate in world exploration and cultural documentation. The August, 1959, issue of our official journal, the *National Geographic Magazine*, tells how our cooperative society in 1916 made possible the preservation of the giant sequoias in California. Our adversaries were the timber barons. They were defeated by the people because there was an organized nonprofit association ready to spend $20,000 of its members' money as a public service. Presently, the Chief Justice of the United States, the President of Pan American Airlines, the President of E. I.

Dupont de Nemours & Co., and other members gladly serve on our board without remuneration. Are these men socialists?

2540 Massachusetts Ave., N. W.: This is the legal name of the cooperative apartment that Mrs. Miller and I have had as a Washington residence since 1945. While our real home and legal domicile is in California, we have found this Washington home a delightful place in which to live. The building has 34 apartments, and each one is assigned to a particular stockholder. Among our fellow members are the retired president of George Washington University, a former ranking executive of the American Telephone and Telegraph Company, a general counsel for the International Business Machines Company, a canon of Washington Cathedral, and two retired generals. Not very "socialistic" neighbors.

Group Health Association: This cooperative was organized some twenty-five years ago by a few Washington, D. C., residents who desired the benefits of clinical medicine and were willing to pay for it. While for many years the American Medical Association opposed it, recently Group Health has been put on the AMA approved list. Group Health practitioners have always been of the highest type and today serve the needs of thousands of families in the Greater Washington area. We have found the services of our group admirably suited to our needs. Group medicine is the antithesis of state-controlled medicine, because all costs are paid by a modest fee, yet some would believe that such groups are "socialistic," perhaps even communistic.

American Automobile Association: The AAA is a service agency operating at cost for over eight million American families. The American Automobile Association has been instrumental in obtaining better roads, creating improved traffic laws, and educating the public in safety precautions. Recently I had occasion to be the guest of the organization's vice president,

A Conservative Looks At Cooperatives

Russell E. Singer, at a Washington country club. Both of us noted with pleasure large numbers of members' cars bearing an AAA emblem. Many of these cars were Cadillacs and Imperials. Surely a strange assortment of "socialists."

Harvard Cooperative Society: Students and faculty members of Harvard purchase supplies and services from this organization at cost. The former Dean of the Business School, Stanley F. Teele, is also a member of the board of directors of such organizations as General Foods, Allegheny Ludlum, and Equitable Life Assurance Society.[8] Rather a strange place to develop a "socialistic" cooperative.

Nationwide Mutual Insurance Company: We carry our automobile and Washington home comprehensive insurance with this organization. Nationwide, which arose through the service given by the Ohio Farm Bureau to its members, has become one of the largest companies in the country dealing in automobile and home insurance. The company's original board of directors was made up for the most part of Ohio farmers. Is this socialism?

Farmers Mutual Insurance Co., Stockton, California: Over fifty years ago, my father and a number of other farmers in San Joaquin County, California, feeling that rates for fire insurance were too high, organized their own mutual fire insur-

[8]*Dean Stanley F. Teele of the Harvard Business School brought the following statement by Mr. R. L. Nowell, of Equitable Life Assurance Society, to my attention: "At the outset let it be clear that we favor the cooperative idea. In fact I could hardly do otherwise because the Equitable Society is one of the largest and most successful cooperatives in the Nation. All of its $4,410,000,000 worth of assets are owned by approximately 3½ million members. All income from the business after deducting expenses and necessary reserves is returned annually to policyholders."*

ance company. They charged one-half the then-existing board rates and had a clause in the policy that if the charge was too low there would be an assessment. To the best of my knowledge there has been only one small assessment in over half a century of operation. This saved money has manifested itself in better homes and farm buildings. Rates are, of course, now on an experienced rating basis. My brother, David, is a director of the company. Its assets are nearly $1,000,000. Not too socialistic!

National Press Club: This cooperative has long been the focal point for world news in Washington. The leaders of the political and business world appear before its members and use this forum to offer important pronouncements. Representatives of all the communication media, including the Associated Press, itself a cooperative, rub elbows at the National Press Club. If this is socialism, make the most of it.

Pacific Mutual Insurance Company: I cannot resist quoting the succinct statement made by this company to its policy holders when it changed from a profit to a nonprofit organization. The benefits accruing to the policyholders are stated with dramatic clarity:

> It is a pleasure to tell you that on July 28, 1959, as one of Pacific Mutual's life insurance policyholders, you became one of the new owners of the company—a company with over two and one-half billions of life insurance in force and with assets approaching six hundred millions of dollars.
> On that date the complete mutualization of the company was accomplished. As a result you have acquired certain rights and we ask you to read this message carefully so that you will be fully informed about these rights and how you may exercise them.
> The mutualization of your company is good news in a dollars-and-cents way. This is because a mutual company returns to its life insurance policyholders, in the

form of policy dividends, surplus earnings not required to conduct the business as a healthy, going concern.

CARE—Cooperative for American Relief Everywhere: CARE is the creation of numerous cooperative, labor, and religious organizations throughout the nation; its objective is to help needy individuals EVERYWHERE. CARE proudly features the word COOPERATIVE on its masthead. This cooperative is owned by a number of nonprofit organizations and incorporated under the Cooperative Corporations Act of the District of Columbia. Each member has one vote on the Board of Directors. The Cooperative League of the USA took the initiative in organizing CARE; Murray Lincoln, president of the League, served also as the president of CARE during its first twelve years of operation.

CARE has done more to give the peoples of the world a proper understanding of the United States than have all the innumerable grants proffered by our government to other governments. CARE encourages self-help. Yes, people working together through their own organization can do what the disciples of Karl Marx have never been able to accomplish.

While CARE because of its corporate structure has as members only voluntary organizations, we, as individuals, can and do utilize its services at cost. Any residue over costs is used for general welfare work overseas.

People Benefit from Existence of Cooperative Organizations

My wife and I belong to several other cooperative groups, but the list is too long to be included here. We get excellent travel service from the American Travel Association, enjoy meeting friends and scholars at the Cosmos Club; our New York business home is the Canadian Club. All of these organizations are at our service because, within our capitalistic economy, people can join together to create groups that serve them at cost.

There are many other areas of service performed for individuals by the nonprofit corporate entity. The list is almost endless but the principle is the same; within the framework of a capitalistic economy, individual people and groups can often attain "economic democracy" through the use of the nonprofit corporate technique.

Cooperatives are a part of our enlightened twentieth-century service capitalism. Probably 90 percent or more of all Americans belong to one or more cooperatives. But the cooperative will not be limited to America alone; the rest of the world will undoubtedly create cooperative ventures of its own. This nonprofit segment of capitalism is not antagonistic to the profit segment. In some areas cooperatives are appropriate, and in other areas private business—both are aspects of capitalism.

Here in North America we have developed the highest standard of living in the history of mankind. Our affluent life is the result of many factors, not the least of which is a free-flowing capitalistic economy. There are no fixed avenues of traffic. In our land, the consumer is king. The consumer may elect to operate his own business, in other words, a cooperative, or, he may choose to leave business to another. Incidentally, it is interesting to note that the creation of a cooperative usually occurs when some profit-making business does its job badly. Cooperatives seldom arise in areas where business is functioning fairly and efficiently.

Ours is a free government ruled by law, and cooperatives —forbidden by law in some countries—are encouraged. Cooperatives reciprocally owe a continuing loyalty to the principles of freedom which gave them birth. Their officers must remember that they are a part of a capitalistic economy, and must strive constantly to improve the services of the organization which they guide; they must be willing to pay hard dollars for research and not leave the financing of research entirely to the states which charter them. The cooperatives need to realize that they must constantly educate their ever-changing membership, for birth and death are ever with us. They must consider ways of attracting and holding second-generation members and managers. They must purchase their goods and services on the market place at market prices and not expect or accept special favors from the business community. And finally, they must make it possible for a cooperative employee to hold his head high in any community without feeling he is engaged in a second-class business.

Yes, cooperatives are a part of Enlightened Capitalism, with all the problems of other forms of American Capitalism, plus one additional problem—the constant education of the members of the cooperative. But this added task is more than just a chore; it is the cooperative's crowning glory. The member of the cooperative is also its customer. No other form of business has such an opportunity to create friendly relationships. We know whether the cooperative is fulfilling its destiny or not by the answer to this simple question: Do we call cooperatives OURS or THEIRS?

THE NONPROFIT CORPORATION OR ASSOCIATION IN THE NON-AGRICULTURAL FIELD

Note: This section was originally written in collaboration with my late law associate, Dr. Herbert R. Grossman.[9] I have deleted some outdated material and added a few new sentences and figures. I could recommend that the student of this phase of the subject study the original publication, if for no other purpose than to become acquainted with the rapid growth of these service organizations in

[9]*Raymond W. Miller and Herbert R. Grossman, in* LAW AND CONTEMPORARY PROBLEMS, *XIII, No. 3 (Summer 1948), 453-472.*

the past fifteen years—the old figures and evaluations are hopelessly outdated.

This section discusses the role of the nonprofit corporation and association in the nonagricultural field. No attempt will be made to cover every type of business; only leading examples will be discussed to bring out instances where the corporation and/or association act as agents or agencies on a nonprofit or cooperative basis primarily for the benefit of their members and patrons. The subject matter thus presented is intended merely as a guidepost, pointing the various directions in which such organizations are moving, but not serving as a recommendation of the direction that business should take.

Corporations have until recently been operated primarily for the pecuniary profit of stockholders.[10] However, beginning with the philosophy of the now famous Rochdale pioneers in England in 1844, as well as earlier mutual aid and joint assurance efforts, a new concept of doing business has developed—business conducted on a mutual nonprofit or cooperative basis. It should be fully recognized that the theory of the nonprofit or cooperative entities is to employ the corporate association as an instrumentality which, making no gain for itself, serves its stockholders or patrons by increasing their profits or lessening their expenses. The chief reason for forming such bodies is to enable individuals or companies to accomplish jointly through the corporate agent what they cannot achieve singly or severally, in competition with each other.

[10]*In the leading case of Dodge v. Ford Motor Company, 204 Mich. 458, 170 N. W. 668 (1919), noted in 17 Mich. Law Rec. 502 (1919), the court stated: "A business corporation is organized and carried on primarily for the profit of the stockholders. The powers of the directors are to be employed for that end. The discretion . . . does not extend to . . . the reduction of profits, or to the non-distribution of profits among stockholders in order to devote them to other purposes." Id. at 684.*

89

The Associated Press[11] and the Canadian Press [12] are two prominent nonprofit corporations, the prime purpose of which is to act as service agents for their members. Banking Clearing House Associations are voluntary, nonprofit, unincorporated associations of member banks existing solely for the purpose of

[11]*See Associated Press v. United States, 326 U. S. 1 (1945). This was a civil action wherein the United States successfully enjoined the Associated Press, composed of newspaper publishers, from combining cooperatively to violate the Sherman Antitrust Act. The opinion of the Court brought out the fact that the publishers of more than 1,200 newspapers comprised the membership of the Associated Press and that it was a nonprofit cooperative association incorporated under the membership corporation law of the state of New York. In the majority opinion, Mr. Justice Black significantly pointed out: "We need not again pass upon the contention . . . that because AP's activities are cooperative, they fall outside the sphere of business . . . . When Congress has desired to permit cooperatives to interfere with the competitive system of business, it has done so expressly by legislation." Id. at 14.*

A statute allowing the formation of corporations not for profit without capital stock is not confined to religious, literary, or charitable corporations, or those of a similar nature, but applies to any corporation not for profit. See, e.g., Read v. Tidewater Coal Exchange, 13 Del. Ch. 195, 116 Atl. 898 (1922) (coal dealer's exchange agency to facilitate coal handling); McClure v. Cooperative Elevator & Supply Co., 103 Kan. 91, 181 Pac. 573 (1919). A "mutual company" is one wherein the members constitute both the insurer and the insured, where the members all contribute, by a system of assessments, to the creation of a fund from which all losses and liabilities are paid, and wherein the profits are divided among themselves in proportion to their interests. State v. Willett, 171 Ind. 296, 86 N.E. 68 (1908). Pennsylvania statutes, similar to those in a great many states, permit the creation of a nonprofit corporation "for any purpose or purposes which are lawful and not injurious to the community." Pub. L. 289, Art. II, g201, May 5, 1933.

[12]*The Canadian Press is a cooperative news-gathering and distributing association of the Canadian daily papers. It is the*

rendering service in the clearing of checks of all banks and for the general welfare of their members. Most of the stock and commodity exchanges throughout the country are nonprofit associations, and, unlike ordinary business corporations, do not operate for pecuniary gain.[13]

The American Institute of Banking, a section of the American Bankers Association, is a voluntary, nonprofit, educational institution. Its objective is to train bank employees in theoretical and practical principles of banking and allied subjects.

Public utilities in the early 1940's found that the nonprofit corporation is a valuable purchasing agent for use by power companies in the joint acquisition of goods. For example, the operating subsidiaries of Engineers Public Service Company (Delaware) obtained economies and more efficient service through group operation of certain essential services, including executive, advisory, purchasing, sales promotion, insurance, accounting, statistical, tax, and corporate services. These services are furnished on a nonprofit basis by Engineers Public Service Company, Inc. (New York), a mutual service organization wholly owned by the operating subsidiaries of Engineers Public Service Company.[14]

Nonprofit contract chain organizations of individually-

first cooperative news association in the Empire. This enterprise sells nothing, makes no profits, declares no dividends, owns no buildings or property except the furniture and fixtures in its bureaus, and is governed by the basic cooperative principle of "one paper—one vote." "The Canadian Press," CANADIAN BUSINESS *(January 1, 1947).*

[13]*Dickinson v. Board of Trade, 114 Ill. A. 295 (1904); Constitution of the New York Stock Exchange, Art. 1, g2,* IN RE *Haebler v. New York Produce Exchange, 149 N. Y. 414, 44 N.E. 87 (1896); White v. Brownell, 3 Abb. Pr. (N.S.) [N.Y]. 318 (1868) (aff'd 2 Daly 329); Crane, Parris & Co. v. Clearing House Ass'n. 2 Pa. Dist. 509 (1893).*

[14]*Financial and Statistical Report for the year 1944, Engineers Public Service Company (Delaware).*

owned stores or small chains have met the competition of the large integrated corporate chain stores. Thousands of independently owned grocery stores have set up central wholesale purchasing nonprofit corporations which have enabled them to compete with the far-flung activities of the single corporate-operated multiple-outlet chain stores.

The North American Indian has gone in for cooperation, too. Indian cooperatives to market the handicraft products of various tribes exist among the Winnebago Indian families in Wisconsin, the Navajos in New Mexico, and the Chippewa Indians in North Dakota.

Currently the Eskimos of Canada are developing several highly successful cooperatives to purchase supplies, maintain product standards, and market their indigenous art and sculpturing work. I have on my desk at this moment an heroic Eskimo carved in stone by one of these craftsmen; it was given to me as a present by the Canadian Public Relations Society, itself a nonprofit service organization.

Millions of American motorists have contributed to the creation of a nonprofit service corporate institution in the American Automobile Association. Having no stockholders, the AAA devotes its revenues to providing a series of specialized services for a large segment of the car-owning public.[15]

In 1945, a group of cooperatives, labor-unions, church and voluntary relief organizations decided that there should be a unified effort in purchasing goods so that individuals in the United States could ship relief packages with guaranteed delivery to specified persons abroad. A committee was appointed to investigate the best way to handle this and, after careful consideration, accepted the plan of Dr. Lincoln Clark for a nonprofit corporate entity (noncharitable). Accordingly, such an organization was set up under the Cooperative Corporations

[15]See Charter and Bylaws of the American Automobile Association, incorporated April 29, 1910, Connecticut.

Act of the District of Columbia with the name of Cooperative for American Remittances to Europe, commonly known as CARE (later changed to Cooperative for American Relief Everywhere). Formerly, single organizations and individuals could not get packages to friends and relatives abroad, except at excessive cost and with extreme hazards. But by the use of this nonprofit corporate device, functioning as a procurement and shipping agent at cost, both individuals and institutions have reaped the benefits of efficient mass distribution, and the world is receiving a demonstration of cooperative private enterprise in action in a capitalistic economy.[16]

Group Health Association, Washington, D. C., is a well-known cooperative operating a clinic and pharmacy and is a monument to the vision of my longtime friend and associate Raymond R. Zimmerman. Originally organized to serve only federal employees, Group Health Association adopted early in 1946 open, racially integrated membership on a group basis.

There are many cemetery and burial associations conducted on a nonprofit basis. In some jurisdictions the declared policy of the law prevents the formation of cemetery associations for the purpose of making a profit. In such states the members cannot make a profit for themselves from the sale of lots or from other revenue of the cemetery, nor can they make a gift of their revenue to another independent corporation.[17]

[16]*"The Cooperative for American Remittances to Europe (CARE) is shipping individual food packages to persons in Europe the cost of which is paid for by donors in this country. CARE operates as a private, nonprofit cooperative food distributor with the sanction and cooperation of the various governments. Its activities are proving daily that the efficiency of private business can be utilized in world relief distribution."* PROCEEDINGS OF THE BOSTON CONFERENCE ON DISTRIBUTION, 1946. See also "C.A.R.E., Inc.," FORTUNE (Dec. 1947), p. 127 ff.

[17]*Brown v. Maplewood Cemetery Assn.*, 85 Minn. 498, 89 N. W. 872 (1902); *Clark v. Rahway Cemetery*, 69 N. J. Eq. 636, 51 Atl. 261 (1905).

A Conservative Looks At Cooperatives

New York City has seen the widest use of cooperative housing in the U. S., thanks partly to favorable city and state laws. Nearly 100,000 cooperative housing units were in existence, under construction, or planned in 1962. Two large organizations, backed by co-op, labor, and civic groups, had developed more than half of these units.

Across the country, Federal Housing Administration had in January, 1962, insured mortgages on 278 housing co-ops with 42,000 members. FHA also had 200 other co-op applications under consideration. Federal National Mortgage Association made some of these loans; conventional lenders financed most of them.

In 1961-62, cooperative housing appeared on the verge of spectacular growth. The 1961 Housing Act encouraged co-ops to help renew the heart of U. S. cities. It also allowed FHA to insure loans at below-market interest to co-ops made up of limited-income families. It further provided direct loans for co-ops designed for elderly people. One such co-op, sponsored by a Bedford, N. Y., church, will have sixty-eight ground-floor apartments with non-skid floors and other safety features. It will cost $985,000.

Also, FHA was stepping up its loans to co-ops of tenants who want to buy out their landlords. With small down payments, these families accumulate equities in their refurbished units, generally paying less each month than they formerly paid in rent.[18]

Students' cooperatives exist on many college campuses for furnishing rooms, meals, and school supplies to students on a nonprofit basis.

Credit unions constitute one of the most popular forms of nonprofit corporations and associations. A credit union is a group of persons, associated in daily life, who agree to form an organization under either state or federal laws for the pur-

[18]Cooperatives USA, 1961-62 (Chicago, 1962), p. 35.

94

pose of building up a fund with their savings in order to make loans, at reasonable interest rates, to members of the group. In some cases, the common bond consists of membership in a church, a labor union, a cooperative, or merely residence in a small rural community. The group usually consists of employees of a single employer, such as workers in an office, store, manufacturing plant, railroad, university, or government agency. Postal Credit Unions (composed of federal postal employees) are an example. There are now 400 such unions.

The first credit union in the United States was established in 1909 in Manchester, New Hampshire. Massachusetts passed the first state credit union law, or enabling act, in the same year. This Massachusetts law is considered the foundation of the organized credit union movement in this country.

Religious bodies and churches have used credit unions extensively. By 1947, 575 credit unions had been formed by the congregations of various churches in the United States and Canada.[19] By 1962 the number had risen to 1,670. About 1,240 of these groups are in Roman Catholic parishes, 410 in Protestant churches, 27 in Jewish congregations, and 11 within a miscellany of other religious groups.

Since 1948, federal credit unions have been chartered and supervised by the Bureau of Federal Credit Unions, now a part of the U. S. Department of Health, Education, and Welfare. In addition to the federal statutes, the laws of forty-four states and the District of Columbia now provide for the chartering of credit unions.

There are over 25,900 credit unions now functioning in the United States and Canada. More than 20,000 of these are in the United States, with over 12,800,000 members; more than $5 billion in savings have been accumulated. About half of the active credit unions in the United States are federally chartered.

[19]Benson Y. Landis, THE CHURCH AND CREDIT UNIONS (pamphlet published by the Federal Council of Churches of Christ in America, 1947).

Credit unions are also known as "cooperative banks" or "people's banks." In Massachusetts, however, the term "Co-operative Banks" signifies incorporated bodies which elsewhere are known as building and loan associations.

Credit unions and commercial banks usually get along well together in our free economy. There is a division of services between the two institutions. Credit unions generally cater to the short-term credit needs of people in the low-income brackets whom the commercial banks do not often serve; furthermore, the credit unions themselves maintain accounts in the banks.

One of the oldest of the people's business organizations is the mutual insurance association. Almost every form of insurance—life, health and accident, automobile, home, furniture, hospital and medical, and fire—is sold by these associations.

Mutual and cooperative savings banks are an important part of the basic financial structure of many states, particularly in the northeastern United States. In many cases these institutions have developed an integrated insurance program in conjunction with a program of safety in savings.

The numerous cooperative electric power companies are spearheaded by the activities of the Rural Electrification Administration.[20] Through self-liquidating loans, REA provides 100 percent financing for constructing rural electric facilities to serve rural people who do not have central station electric service. The law provides that, in making such loans, prefer-

[20]*The REA was created by Executive Order No. 7037 of May 11, 1935, under authority of the Emergency Relief Appropriation Act of 1935, approved April 8, 1935 (49 Stat. 115). Statutory provision for the agency was made in the Rural Electrification Act of May 20, 1936 (49 Stat. 1363, 7 U.S.C. gg901-914). It was made a part of the federal Department of Agriculture in 1935. In 1944 Congress liberalized the terms of REA loans and removed the time limitation from its lending program (58 Stat. 739, 7 U.S.C. g903 [Supp. 1946]).*

ence shall be given to public bodies, cooperatives, and nonprofit or limited-dividend associations.[21]

As early as the 1940 census there were 4,356 mutual non-profit irrigation companies in the country. Where there is no offer to the public and the service is extended only to certain individuals as a matter of accommodation or for particular reasons, the supplying of water for irrigation is not deemed a public use. Accordingly, a mutual cooperative water company is not subject to the jurisdiction of a public utility commission, nor may it exercise the prerogative of eminent domain.[22]

The radio cooperative is a newcomer to nonprofit enterprise. Ohio's farmers long protested against what they considered hurried and inadequate radio programs. Accordingly, WRFD, Ohio's first rural radio station, was created, backed by more than 55,000 members of the Ohio Farm Bureau Federation. The station began serving the farmers on September 27, 1947.[23]

[21]*United States Government Manual (2nd ed., Government Information Service, Office of Government Reports: Washington, D.C., 1947).*
[22]*DePauw University v. Public Service Commission of Oregon, 247 Fed. 183 (D. Ore. 1917), 253 Fed. 848 (D. Ore. 1918); Southern California Edison Co. v. Railroad Commission of California, 194 Cal. 757, 230 Pac. 661 (1924). See also the Carey Act, 41 Stat. 1085 (1921), as amended, 43 U.S.C. g641 ET SEQ. (1940). It has been held that a nonprofit cooperative corporation supplying electric service to its members only is not a public service corporation and therefore not subject to regulation by the Commission. Inland Empire Rural Electrification v. Department of Public Service of Washington, 199 Wash. 527, 92 P. 2d 258 (1939); Garkane Power Co. v. Public Service Commission, 98 Utah 466, 100 P. 2d 571 (1940); Department of Public Utilities v. R. O. McConnell, 198 Ark. 502, 130 S.W. 2d 9 (1939); William Meade Fletcher,* CYCLOPEDIA OF THE LAW OF PRIVATE CORPORATIONS *g68 ET SEQ. (Perm. ed. 1931).*
[23]NEWS FOR FARMER COOPERATIVES *(Jan. 1948), p. 5.*

Throughout this discussion reference has been made to various nonprofit businesses as "corporations." It should be remembered that in many instances such businesses are not incorporated, but function under various statutes as "associations," "societies," and the like, enjoying a quasi-corporate status.[24] The use of the word "association" or "society" gives no indication as to whether the business is incorporated or not. For the most part, however, these organizations are incorporated.

The nonprofit commercial corporation is not a panacea for the ills of business. It must be operated as efficiently as a profit corporation because it definitely is an agent acting in the role of securing individual profits or savings for its members. It is, however, a lawful agency which a multitude of individuals, partnerships, and corporations may effectively and profitably use in the performance of a part of their business activities. It should be viewed as a corporate tool to be used jointly with others when needed. If an organization is large enough to handle its own off-premise business in such a way as to meet competition and secure volume prices, then there is no need for it to become part of any nonprofit corporate venture. On the other hand, the American economy is largely predicated upon small ownership and individual operation of businesses. In servicing medium-sized operations, it is increasingly important to utilize the nonprofit corporation to obtain for the individual units the efficiency and service enjoyed by members of a mass-integrated organization. This peculiarly democratic corporation may be used in such a manner that individual ownership and operation of home and business will

[24]*For the story of a successful nonagricultural association, see* Flowers-by-Wire *(Florist Telegraph Delivery Association: Detroit, Mich.).*

See also All About Candy and Chocolate *(Chicago, Ill., 1958), the history and growth since 1884 of the National Confectioners' Association of the United States, Inc.*

be made more attractive and secure. Many large corporations also find that the public can be better served by using such a joint corporate structure for certain services which would be too costly if performed severally.

One of the best defenses of the American businessman against the inroads of undue state regulation lies in the joint use of a corporation created to serve as agent, without profit, in the rendering of essential services which he can neither afford individually nor accomplish independently.

V. Cooperatives Around The World

"Rural people are the backbone of the world's economy. Because cooperative organization is such an important means to essential ends, both IFAP and FAO are deeply interested in progress in this field."

"More emphasis should be placed on assisting the rural people to organize cooperative associations. The little farmer, left alone, even with a good crop, is something of an economic derelict. But farmers working together along cooperative lines become a force for the creation of a better life for themselves and their families."

FAO AND COOPERATIVES

Cooperative organization can be used to increase production, improve distribution, raise the level of the world's farmers, fishermen, and foresters.[1]

Rural people are the backbone of the world's economy. Cooperatives help to strengthen that backbone. Because cooperative organization is such an important means to essential ends, both IFAP (International Federation of Agricultural Producers) and FAO (Food and Agricultural Organization) are deeply interested in the development of cooperatives.

[1]*This and the following paragraphs are from a statement by Raymond W. Miller, Consultant on Cooperatives on behalf of Norris E. Dodd, Director-General of the Food and Agriculture Organization of the United Nations, at the meeting of the International Federation of Agricultural Producers, Guelph, Canada, May, 1949. The policies described are still followed by FAO.*

A Conservative Looks At Cooperatives

FAO Policy on Cooperatives

FAO has no fixed formula as to how cooperatives should be formed or managed, except that they must be in the public interest and adapted to local needs and cultures. Cooperatives are the direct antithesis of statism and are an effective agency not only for economic services but for promoting education and a higher standard of living. The world must recognize that the dignity of man is increased by helping man to help himself— which is the objective of cooperatives.

The 4th Session of the FAO Conference, held in November, 1948, adopted as part of its recommended program for FAO the following principles:

> The Conference considers that cooperative societies provide one of the best means of reducing the cost of farm production supplies, credit and marketing, reducing the price of consumer goods to all people, and developing crop insurance and other forms of mutual aid which will enable rural populations to improve production and conditions of life.

> The Conference therefore commends FAO for the start made in the field of cooperatives, and welcomes the proposal to hold a conference of workers with practical experience in cooperatives in the Far East during 1949; recommends that similar conferences be held in other regions as requested; and further, that the work of FAO on farm credit, marketing, and consumers' and other types of cooperatives be expanded by providing a consultative service to member governments on methods of aiding and developing such cooperative programs, both through the central and regional FAO offices. For this purpose, the Conference urges the Director-General to consider the possibility of adding technically qualified personnel to the staff to work with the FAO divisions concerned in the promotion of cooperative activities, and to secure, if necessary, authorization from the Council of FAO for the necessary transfer of funds. In this program FAO should consult and cooperate with the International

Labour Organization, and International Federation of Agricultural Producers, and International Cooperative Alliance.

These recommendations are being implemented, and the FAO stands ready to work with existing agencies throughout the world in the accomplishment of such a program.

Ways FAO Will Implement Objective

In accordance with the outlined objective, FAO established a consultative service on cooperatives, and informal discussions have been held in several South Asian and North American countries. Others will follow as quickly as funds are available and requests for such meetings are received from various member governments. The conference of workers with practical experience in cooperatives, mentioned in the first of the above quoted paragraphs, was held in Southeast Asia in late October, 1949.

FAO hopes that it can be of material assistance to cooperatives by thus conferring directly with rural leaders, educators, and government officials in the areas involved. [Note: In the intervening years, FAO has, each year, done more work with member governments to encourage the development of cooperatives.]

While FAO is an association of governments, the International Federation of Agricultural Producers is a free association of the organized farmers of the world working together for mutual benefit and public good.

Many of a farmer's best tools are two-man tools, like the cross-cut saws which farmers often use to cut up their winter supplies of fuel. The development and use of cooperatives to help undertake the great jobs which confront us all is peculiarly like these two-man jobs of the farmer. Government in all countries, with FAO, can pull one end of the saw. Those in IFAP can pull the other end. Between them they can cut the log.

103

Working together in this way is particularly necessary in the development of cooperatives. Government powers can create the conditions under which cooperatives can rise and flourish. But cooperatives are in their essence free associations of individuals working with each other to do for themselves things which they cannot do so well, or cannot do at all, alone. Perhaps by failing to create the proper conditions, government could prevent cooperatives from succeeding. But government cannot make a cooperative work unless the people who compose it want to work and understand how to make it work.

There is among farmers, therefore, a great educative and organizing task, which only government and the FAO can undertake. However, government and FAO will constantly need advice as they endeavor to help farmers.

Everywhere we observe that the organizations of rural people have established enviable reputations for sound and responsible action. This being so, it is natural that we should see governments everywhere turning to farmer organizations for advice on measures affecting the interests of rural people. Had it not been for rural people, there would have been no FAO. It was they who made it clear to government that such an agency was necessary.

How IFAP Can Contribute to Cooperative Development

There are four principal ways through which IFAP can contribute to the development of cooperative organization:

First, it can intensify the organizing and educative work which constituent bodies of IFAP are already carrying on among rural people in many countries.

Second, it can keep FAO advised on (a) problems which have been successfully solved through cooperatives, (b) problems which require solution.

Third, it can cooperate with member governments in utilizing FAO's consultative service on cooperatives.

Finally, it can advise with cooperative leaders, educators, government officials and others on activities of the FAO cooperative consultative service that it may be of the greatest possible benefit to the countries concerned.

FAO stands ready to render whatever service it can, and looks to the International Federation of Agricultural Producers for continuing advice, counsel, and assistance.

Cooperatives in Asian Countries

A technical meeting on cooperatives was held in 1949 at Lucknow, India. Dr. Horace Belshaw, Director of the Rural Welfare Division of the Food and Agricultural Organization of the United Nations, prepared a report on this well-attended meeting. [2] The report is available and well worth study by those interested in the international aspects of cooperatives.

People of the East Agree on Value of Cooperatives

At the Lucknow meeting it became clear that the people of the East consider the use of cooperatives of great assistance in raising the standard of living of their agricultural workers. The method of operation of a cooperative may differ in various parts of the world, but the principle and the purpose are the same everywhere.

"Let There Be Bread"

FAO's motto is "Fiat Panis." The translation of this Latin phrase is "Let There Be Bread," and to FAO "bread" means the products of farms, fisheries, and forests. Until there is bread for all, we cannot expect a peaceful world. Forty-two governments ratified FAO's constitution when the organization was founded in October 1945; there are now 111 member governments. The preamble to FAO's constitution states in a few words the new cooperative approach to world problems based on human need. It reads:

[2]"Report of Technical Meeting on Cooperatives in Asia and the Far East, Lucknow, India, October 24-November 2, 1949," FAO, 1201 Connecticut Avenue, N. W., Washington, D.C.

The Nations accepting this Constitution, being determined to promote the common welfare by furthering
separate and collective action on their part for the purposes of
> Raising levels of nutrition and standards of
> living of the peoples under their respective ju-
> risdictions,
> Securing improvements in the efficiency of the
> production and distribution of all food and
> agricultural products,
> Bettering the conditions of rural populations,
> and thus contributing toward an expanding
> world economy,

Hereby establish the Food and Agriculture Organization
of the United Nations . . . through which the Members
will report to one another on the measures taken and
the progress achieved in the fields of action set forth
above.

Ten Meals Away from Savagery!

The net world population gain approaches 7,500 human
beings per hour, 180,000 human beings in a twenty-four hour
period—figures which challenge the imagination and the
world's resources. In the twentieth century there is a race between man and starvation. FAO, as a cooperative of its Member Governments, is attempting to eliminate hunger through
the collection, distribution, and implementation of scientific
knowledge. Never before has there been any comparable effort
to help men help themselves to a full plate of food. The staff
of FAO, although small in number, has learned how to multiply
its effect by demonstrating to people in many countries the
means of taking the knowledge of the world and using it cooperatively.

Inducing Cooperative Effort in Asia

*Small holdings and archaic marketing and purchasing
methods combine in most areas to make the lot of the*

*primary producers—the farmers—one of almost predes-
tined poverty. An effective policy of American help to
meet this situation would encourage cooperatives.*[3]

In all areas where they have been tested, voluntarily organized cooperatives have proved that they can assist in producing better rural life, if honestly and efficiently operated in
the public interest. The cooperative is a necessary follow-up to
land reform. The great work of the MacArthur administration
in Japan illustrates this quite clearly. The far-reaching, step-
by-step program of land reform accomplished in Japan in the
five years after World War II has already been mentioned; in
Japan the large estates were split up and sold to the farmers,
who obtained on the average between two and five acres each.
Cooperatives become necessary when farms that small are the
norm. Buying for himself, the small farmer finds he cannot
afford the fertilizer for his crop or improved farm implements;
practices such as forward buying are virtually out of the question. The lot of the private fisherman is no easier. The resulting
widespread demand for forming cooperatives that followed was,
fortunately, supported by the administration. As a result, farm
and fishing cooperatives exist in practically every village and
fishing cove in Japan.

In the Philippines, in 1951 the possibilities of the cooperative purchasing of plows and other items hold out a main source
of hope for modernizing the primitive agriculture that prevails in
many sections. A series of fifty-four seminars on cooperatives
held in the Philippine Islands indicates the value which government leaders have come to place on such associations.

The method of operation of a cooperative may differ in
various parts of the world, but the principle is the same and
so is the purpose. In many sections, industrial cooperatives may

[3] *This and the following paragraphs are from Raymond W.
Miller, "Our Economic Policy in Asia,"* HARVARD BUSINESS
REVIEW *(July 1951), 60 ff.*

be seen in their most primary forms. For example, handicraft and fish net cooperatives, with backing from a central agency, pool small sums to buy the raw materials with which to manufacture their products. Pooling arrangements are used for selling the products. A village cooperative may start with as little as $10 borrowed capital (with a "mere" 10 percent interest charge for three months' use), buying twine in fairly reasonable quantities to make fish nets. The cooperative members make standard nets and sell them at a profit, which may be three or four times larger than it would have been if there had been no cooperative. To be sure, it may take a girl ten hours to make a net selling for the American equivalent of about 25 cents, and she may have to pay 20 percent to 100 percent interest on the cost of the twine, but she is relatively well off when one considers that the annual per capita income of the great masses in China, for instance, averages an estimated $36 per person, and in Japan $100.[4] A few cents more or less means a great deal at that level of living. [Ed. note. The foregoing figures were accurate for 1951 and represented the extreme poverty of these peoples at that time.]

In summary, no American policy of helping Asia effectively at the grass-roots level should underrate the importance of promoting and assisting cooperatives:

> Such things have a tremendous appeal to the Burma peasant wading in the mud of his rice paddy and paying 51 percent of what he produces for the privilege of using his land and paying from 30 to 60 percent interest for his fertilizer, seed, and grocery credit. It might be one way that America could let the little fellow who never hears our Voice of America broadcasts understand that Democracy has something for the little man.[5]

[4]Stanley Andrews, "Cooperatives as Builders of Democracy," News for Farmer Cooperatives (November 1950), 13-14.
[5]Ibid., p. 14.

GREATER EMPHASIS SHOULD BE PLACED ON THE FORMATION OF FARMER COOPERATIVES IN LATIN AMERICA

As consultants to people in other lands, American technicians can literally move mountains. But if the government of the United States is involved as one of the principals, the situation is altered. Latin Americans do not enjoy submitting to direction from the outside. The use of the finest technical knowledge in the world can boomerang if the self esteem of the people being helped is disregarded.[6]

Participation in Cooperative Enterprises, Such as Farm Machinery Pools, Should Be Re-examined

Because we want to get things done, we sometimes act hastily. Cooperatives have evolved slowly in the United States; they did not spring to life full grown. *We do not help the Latin American farmer to help himself by providing him with things that he had no part in building up himself, such as farm machinery pools.*

As soon as possible, the direct participation of the United States in actual cooperative enterprises, whether through *servicios*[7] or otherwise, should be examined. A rule of thumb that

[6]*This and the following paragraphs are from a "Report on Public Relations Audit of the United States Technical Cooperation Program in Latin America," undertaken for the Technical Cooperation Administration by Raymond W. Miller, CONGRESSIONAL RECORD (May 13, 1953); summarized in "Making Point Four Work," HARVARD BUSINESS SCHOOL BULLETIN (Winter 1954).*

[7]*The SERVICIO is the operating agency which does the work of the Point Four program in Latin America. It is an integral part of the appropriate ministry in the government of the Latin American country. It is substantially similar to a bureau in one of the departments of the government of the United States. The Director of the SERVICIO is usually the Chief of Field Party sent by the Institute of Inter-American Affairs to the particular country to represent the United States in the*

might be followed is that only those enterprises should be undertaken that the Land-Grant colleges and Extension Services have found practical in their work with the states. Farmers are the same the world over. We should encourage Latin Americans to organize for themselves. When the work is done *for* them, whether it be through *servicios* or other expedients, development of local initiative is defeated and the growth of local leadership retarded.

Latin America lacks adequate rural cooperative leadership and until this leadership is developed the desired goals will not be attained. To the extent that too many or the wrong kind of facilities are provided, the day of attainment is postponed. It would certainly be better to take a few years longer and build indigenously and permanently, rather than through a "flash" operation. I do not refer, however, to such things as small experimental stations and demonstration centers; they are a different matter.

The *servicio* farm machinery enterprises, although small in themselves, should be encouraged to become farmer cooperative organizations. Their most valuable function, that of training operations, could be transferred to experiment stations.

Greater Emphasis Should Be Placed on the Formation of Farmer Cooperatives

Farmer cooperatives have helped to lead the farmers of the United States and of many other countries to prosperity. They have shown that voluntary cooperative effort promotes the general welfare.

There are some successful cooperatives in Latin America

cooperative program. He serves simultaneously in two capacities. He is Director of the Servicio, *answerable to the Minister of the Latin American country, and also Chief of Field Party, answerable to the Institute. Some of his principal staff members and the technicians working with him are United States citizens; the others are nationals of Latin American countries.*

but they are few and far between. I found an exceptionally good one in Brazil; it had been developed by Japanese-Brazilians. And in Colombia the coffee growers cooperatively established one of the finest agricultural experiment stations in the world. The United States helped out with one technician, Dr. Matthew Drosdoff of the University of Florida, who acted as advisor. He helped the Colombians with special problems and did an extraordinarily good job in human relations. As soon as the Colombians were able to carry on without his assistance he would, of course, withdraw from the picture. The establishment of this experiment should be studied and the lessons learned there incorporated into other programs.

One thing is clear: more emphasis should be placed on assisting rural people to organize cooperative associations. The little farmer, left alone, even with a good crop, is something of an economic derelict. *But farmers working together along cooperative lines become a force for the creation of a better life for themselves and their families.*

Establishment of Thrift-Loan Associations of the Credit Union Type Should Be Urged

One of the ways of assisting people economically is to give them the ideas and incentive *to secure needed capital for themselves* by establishing their own credit unions. They must be shown that they possess resources and facilities comparable to private and governmental loan agencies. In some cases, grants for a specific project may be necessary but too great a readiness to provide funds through outside grants could easily weaken the effect of an assistance program. Millions of American families are benefited by the use of credit unions. Rural credit institutions are sadly needed in Latin America.

I spent a little time in a desert community in Peru where some poor tenant farmers (about 140 families) had managed to save the equivalent of about $6,000; with this capital they purchased a truck and some picks and shovels. With the as-

sistance of the *servicio* (which was supplying surveyors and
other technical knowledge) they were digging an irrigation ditch
through a boulder-infested area, and reclaiming usable land
from the desert. What credit associations would do for such
people! When I visited these men at their work, I found not
lethargic peasants, but a group of enthusiastic workers who
showed me with great pride the ditch they were digging. When
I was about to leave they gathered and shouted, "Viva Amer-
icano!" I realized that they were not cheering me but the country that was trying to help them to help themselves.

In Jamaica under the leadership of Rev. John P. Sullivan,
S.J., of St. George's College Extension School, Kingston, there
is being developed a credit union which is worthy of study by
all interested in the growth of such associations in Latin America.[8]

COOPERATIVES IN INDIA

The people of India have an inclination toward cooperative effort. The long history of cooperation by the people in
carrying out the decisions of the *panchayats*[9] is a case in point.

[8]*See Benson Y. Landis, "Churches and Credit Unions,"* IN-
FORMATION SERVICE, *LXI, No. 13 (National Council of the
Churches of Christ in the United States of America, June 23,
1962), 5.*
[9]PANCHAYATS *are a unique, local, self-governing body indigenous to India. The first serious attempt to make panchayats
the bed rock of life of the village community in India started
only in 1950 when a specific directive was laid down under
Article 40 of the Constitution to organize village panchayats
and to confer on them such power and authority as were
necessary to enable them to function as units of local self-
government.*

*Thus, surely and securely, the foundation was laid on
which may stand, in time, self-governing institutions of the
people in every village in India managing every aspect of administration and development of the respective areas them-*

The success of the *panchayats* depends largely upon the voluntary cooperation of the village people.[10]

There is Nothing so Powerful as an Idea Whose Time Has Come

Man is able to cooperate; throughout history there are examples which prove this. One such example is the establishment of credit unions, or, as they are sometimes called, poor man's banks. Some fifty years ago Edward A. Filene observed on a trip to India how the Bombay Thrift Clubs operated; groups of poor laborers saved their annas and created small banks from which they borrowed as need arose.[11] Filene realized immediately organizations of this sort in North America would help raise the economic level of the poor, debt-ridden laborer. Today, some 20 million Americans belong to credit unions; on deposit in these unions are 5 billion dollars. Their loan delinquency rate, it should be noted, is but 1/5 of 1 percent for all loans made. No wonder they are regarded as one of the marvels of the financial world.

However, India, which supplied the inspiration for credit

selves, drawing, if necessary, upon the State only for technical and financial assistance. By providing the base for practicing it at the grass-roots, these "little republics" will indeed make democracy an abiding faith and a living force for the Nation. Definition supplied by the Information Service of India, Embassy of India, Washington, D.C., April 7, 1959.

[10]*This and following paragraphs are from Chapter V, written by Raymond W. Miller and published in* REPORT ON SMALL INDUSTRIES IN INDIA *by the International Planning Team, The Ford Foundation. Published by Ministry of Commerce and Industry, Government of India, 1954.*

[11]*Many writers credit the Raiffeisen cooperative movement in Germany, transplanted to India, as giving Filene this inspiration; but according to many students of cooperatives in India, the idea is really much older and came from the Bombay indigenous workers' thrift clubs.*

unions, was not itself ready for more than a modest beginning in cooperative efforts in the first part of this century. The situation is somewhat different now. The new India is committed to industrial change. The Five-Year Plan and projects such as that in the Damodar Valley will eventually bring industry to even the villages and smaller cities. We have already learned —our experiences from Ireland to Japan prove it—that local and small industry spring up wherever there is electrification. India's millions need industrial products in vast quantities. As these needs are filled, the prosperity of India will grow at a constantly accelerating pace. In the past, Indian cooperatives have thrived best among farmers or in small communities. But to imagine an industrial India without cooperation is to ignore the basic economic factors of the present.[12]

The India Constitution states, Part IV, "The State shall endeavor to promote cottage industries on an individual or cooperative basis in rural areas." Also, in the Constitution, in the Seventh Schedule, List 2 (State List), Article 32, it is specifically mentioned that cooperatives are to be chartered by State Governments. Cooperatives, it can be seen, are part of basic government policy.

While the national directive only mentions cooperatives in relation to cottage industries, it is a generally accepted belief of the people that the national Government has been, is, and will be committed to a policy of encouraging all types of legitimate cooperatives.

Cooperatives of All Types Are Considered

The following basic principles of cooperatives should be recognized, studied, and applied wherever possible.

1. Cooperatives Should Be Used for Credit: Lack of credit was one of the almost unanimous complaints from small indus-

[12]See "Co-op. Farming Makes Little Headway," THE HINDU WEEKLY REVIEW (October 7, 1963), p. 10.

trialists in all Indian communities. However, in some of these communities there is enough idle capital to form the nucleus of successful cooperative financing institutions. Small enterprises should be encouraged to form cooperative credit associations with a minimum of direct government participation. The Reserve Bank of India has the means and facilities for active help in such efforts. Concurrently, the regular banking institutions must enlarge and widen their rural facilities for the handling of accounts and the physical depositing of money. There are cooperatives with no banking facilities available whose officers must go many miles by bus to deposit or withdraw small amounts of money. The creation of mobile cooperative banking units with a circuit of villages is a partial answer. With new roads and communications, such mobile units are possible, particularly in view of the commonly accepted value placed upon law and order in the rural areas.

2. Cooperatives Should Be Used as Procurement Agents for Their Members: The smaller industrial enterpriser is at a distinct disadvantage in the procurement of goods. He often buys at retail and sells at wholesale. The small individual operator often cannot get the quality of raw material he needs to manufacture an acceptable product. The Indian craftsman is reliable and extremely dexterous when given proper tools, but under existing procurement methods he cannot turn out a good product. He should join with other fellow craftsmen to form a cooperative to purchase for himself on order—not on speculation. The cooperative should always purchase for cash and its members should buy from it for cash. The credit cooperative or commercial bank can provide credit facilities. The technical institute program should be of immediate and invaluable service to these procurement cooperatives by aiding them to determine the type and quality of material to be purchased.

3. Marketing Cooperatives Are Often a Necessity If the Small Industrialist Is to Compete Beyond His Local Market: For goods sold locally there may not be any great need for a

marketing cooperative. However, when the goods are sold outside the community a marketing cooperative may be necessary. The industrial marketing cooperative has a much harder task to perform than either the finance or procurement one. A few general principles should be kept in mind. The cooperative should never buy from its producer members. It should accept members' goods on consignment and sell them. Advances should be made on delivery with further payments as the goods are sold. Members of a marketing cooperative must accept the need for the cooperative and accept it as their sole selling agent. If this principle is not followed the cooperative will not work because, in the main, it will be allowed to market the best quality only in times of surplus. A fixed estimate of selling costs should be retained at a high enough level to cover anticipated costs, including market promotion. At the end of predetermined periods, there should be either a refund of overcharges or an assessment of undercharges.

The profitable marketing of the industrial products of India's village and small-scale manufacturers presents some serious and difficult problems. The single operator is at a distinct disadvantage in competing for markets even a few miles away, because the costs involved are too high in proportion to his output. Through cooperative effort, this problem can be solved. The result will be better quality goods at a lower price for the consumer and survival for the manufacturer.

4. Cooperatives Should Stand on Their Own Feet: Governments should create a legal, economic, and political climate which will foster the growth of cooperatives. This does not mean subsidizing. Subsidies are usually a premium on inefficiency and a tax on the consumer. In fact, the subsidized cooperative is too often merely a way of gaining special privileges for the few. The government can, however, always help cooperators to gain experience and confidence by partially participating in cooperative ventures by making available in the initial stages capital, loans, and advisory and managerial service. Cooperatives thrive

where the government acts as a regulator-referee. In India, through a governmentally controlled Reserve Bank, an adequate structure for the financial help needed by cooperatives from outside capital is provided. Grants should not be given —only loans.

Because illiteracy is so widespread in India, people have felt that the government must govern and run the cooperatives. Nothing is farther from the truth. Illiteracy has little to do with intelligence. Successful cooperatives have been run by a preponderately illiterate membership. These succeeded by their own efforts, with the government Registrar acting as guide, friend, and advisor rather than as operator.

It has been found, however, that an alarming number of members of cooperatives believe that the government owns the cooperatives. They refer to the organization as "theirs" and not "ours." Fundamentally, this problem can be solved by withdrawal of the government from a paternalistic and functional attitude towards them.

5. Cooperatives Should Be of the Limited Liability Type: Few industrialists—large or small—will willingly join a cooperative that does not guarantee limited liability. Unlimited or excessive liability tends to keep the provident and the thrifty out and to bring into the cooperative less desirable members. There may have been a time when such arrangements were needed, but that day has passed in the New India. Cooperative insurance and other devices have eliminated the need for unlimited or excessive liability. Cooperatives should develop the self-respect of their members and not make these members feel like second-class borrowers. Coupled with this should be an adequate appraisal of the financial obligation accepted by each member.

6. Cooperators Need Education: One of the greatest handicaps to successful industrial cooperation in India is the lack of facilities for the training of cooperative leaders and managers in the fundamentals of the business organization.

A CONSERVATIVE LOOKS AT COOPERATIVES

The Reserve Bank of India and some cooperative leaders have recently embarked upon a plan to train selected men from cooperatives and government employees from cooperative departments. This is a good plan and it should be furthered so that even a larger number of executives of cooperatives and men from cooperative departments of the government can attend. Of equal importance should be the inauguration of a program to train cooperators themselves. If much of the money and effort now spent by government in promoting the formation of cooperatives could be eliminated and transferred to education in the fundamentals of cooperation and cooperative management, much good would result.

7. Seminars and Short-Term Schools for Cooperatives Should Be Started in Every State of the Land: Cooperative management and organization are so complicated that effective leaders can be developed only through a program of serious study. The lack of education in the fundamentals of cooperation has contributed to the failure of a number of cooperatives in India. Through the various governments, central and state, immediate steps should be taken to work with all cooperative groups to launch cooperative educational programs in all areas of the nation. Thousands from the rank and file of cooperators and potential members of cooperatives need basic education in the principles and practices of cooperation. This should be provided within the area in which they live. Pioneer work in this regard has been done in other countries, with astounding results in cooperative morale and service. In Ceylon there is a cooperative educational program, under which men devoted to cooperative effort can study further and receive encouragement. Denmark, through the inspiration of its People's High Schools, has been among the leaders of the world in this regard. Its system might well be adapted to India in the development of an integral program of better village and cooperative life.

There are many highly qualified men in India who have gone abroad, to Denmark and Canada in particular, to study cooperative education. Unfortunately, the knowledge gained by these men is often lost to cooperatives, since in some cases they have retired a few months after returning, and in others there has been no opportunity to make the knowledge gained available to India. There are also some excellent young men who have gained a thorough education in economics and business administration abroad and who are today frustrated because they cannot find places to employ their knowledge. From this group a fine corps of experts can be selected to superintend the basic education that is so badly needed. People often think that all education requires is a host of large buildings. This notion is, of course, false. A good educational system requires above all informed and devoted teachers. Fortunately, there are a sufficient number of qualified men to carry on the task of teaching the essentials of cooperation.

The money now used for subsidies should be spent on education. An educational program should be established for the villages and outlying areas. This program should be co-ordinated with work done by the Community Projects Administration. It was discovered at Antigonish, Canada, that a thorough study of cooperative principles must precede the formation of cooperatives by at least a year. Hence, no new cooperatives should be formed before primary instruction has been carried out. To obtain personnel to carry out the required educational program, a list of residents of India who have studied cooperation should be made. In addition, a catalogue of the various cooperative educational plans should be prepared. Here is work that the government can undertake to assist the cooperatives without subsidizing them. The Province of Saskatchewan in Canada has successfully set up just such a program. An investment of this sort begun by the Government of India will more than pay for its cost. Not only will cooperatives be developed, but the men who participate in them will grow intellectually and morally. For, as Dr. Paul Manniche of Denmark has said, cooperation is itself an education.

8. Research and Service Department for Cooperatives: In addition to the research and statistical work being done by the Reserve Bank in India, consideration should be given to forming a district organization to function as a clearinghouse for cooperative information.

One of the main functions of such an organization would be to make information available to those organizing a new cooperative. A cooperative without access to basic information tends to wither. Moreover, in India there is a tendency for the people to think that all the good cooperatives are to be found in foreign countries. Actually there are a number of good ones in India itself. Those founding new cooperatives should know of these and be encouraged by their success. The passing on of this information would be another of the tasks of the research and service department I have proposed. The department should immediately on its founding prepare a loose leaf book in which would be kept the histories of the most successful cooperatives in India. The work should be constantly enlarged as new successes are discovered. A representative from this research and service department should move about the country and observe the cooperatives in action. When successful ones are found, they should be studied and the information obtained should be made available to a small board of review, consisting of officers from the various cooperative and *panchayat* associations. The final report should be printed and disseminated.

9. Government Should Gradually Withdraw from Direct Organizations of Cooperatives: Cooperatives must be organized and developed by those who are to be served. They alone must found cooperatives, not the government operating according to an arbitrary timetable. Government, however, does have an important educative function, but should gradually withdraw from the actual operation of specific cooperatives. Cooperation is essentially a people's movement.

One of the great immediate tasks facing the cooperatives is public relations. Cooperatives are considered parasitic by

120

many. It is imperative that the thinking public be correctly informed of the role of cooperatives. Moreover, people interested in joining cooperatives are often discouraged from doing so by hostile critics in the business community who speak only of the cooperatives that have failed. The combatting of such prejudice must be assumed by the cooperators and the government jointly. If the cooperative movement is to grow as it should, public opinion must be on its side. There is no doubt in my mind that the antagonism felt for cooperatives can be dissipated, but this alteration in public feeling can only be achieved by disseminating the facts, both good and bad. Our public relations will fail if we falsify the truth and issue fanciful, over-optimistic propaganda.

10. Cooperatives Are in the Public Interest: Cooperatives have received a great deal of attention from the United Nations Food and Agricultural Organization. I quote from a policy statement made for the Director-General of FAO in May 1949:

> FAO has no formula as to how cooperatives should be formed or managed, except that they must be in the public interest and adapted to local needs and cultures. They are the direct antithesis of statism and are an effective agency not only for economic services but for promoting education and a higher standard of living. The world must recognize that the dignity of man is increased by helping man to help himself—which is the objective of cooperatives.

The Cooperative—A Vertebra of Democracy

Cooperativa Cafeteros De Puerto Rico, now thirty years old, has reached maturity. This organization, led by Ramiro Colon, has won the respect of cooperators everywhere.[13]

In 1950, I recommended that Ernesto Parial, Chief of the

[13]*This and the following paragraphs are from an address by Raymond W. Miller at the annual meeting of the Cooperativa Cafeteros De Puerto Rico, Ponce, Puerto Rico, September 14, 1958.*

A Conservative Looks At Cooperatives

Publicity Division, Cooperatives Administration of the Philippines, visit and study this organization. After his investigation, Mr. Parial returned to his own country and helped in the founding of the now famous *Facoma* (community cooperatives).

Public Relations Audit

In 1952 and 1953, using the members of Public Relations Research Associates as advisers, I made a Public Relations audit of Latin America for the Technical Cooperation Administration of the United States Department of State. Puerto Rico was then moving toward Commonwealth status. I saw Puerto Rico break from the past and emerge into the present. At that time I was certain Puerto Rico, along with Hawaii, had a unique service to perform not only for the United States but also for the free world as a whole. Having studied many of the problems of the newly developing nations of the world at first hand, I was convinced that only by self-help and mutual trust can peace be achieved. My conclusions were presented to the Foreign Affairs Committee of the Congress and are included in the *Congressional Record* of May 13, 1953. I said, among other things:

> We can be proud of Puerto Rico. It is, by Act of Congress and the consent of its own electorate, a Commonwealth of the United States of America. Puerto Ricans are loyal, industrious Americans and are willingly assuming the responsibilities of citizenship. The island is making great progress in industrialization on the local community level and has developed over 150 new industries within the past few years.
>
> Puerto Rico offers great possibilities as a potential "briefing center" for our field personnel bound for assignments in Latin America, and provides a case study in the working of democracy for students from all of the Americas—North, Central, and South—as well as from abroad. We should make use of it in these connections.

Puerto Ricans are engaged in the battle of ideas to win

understanding from their fellow men; some of their most notable victories have been in the field of cooperation. I am proud to be associated with them in their battle of cooperatives.

Ten Questions

A real cooperator can be judged by ten standards. He can judge himself—he needs no other evaluation. These ten standards are as follows:

1. Am I Loyal?

By belonging to a cooperative, I have voluntarily assumed certain obligations. Among these is loyalty. I know that my cooperative is only as strong as its membership and that it needs my full support. If I am loyal, I do not believe every story I hear about the organization. I know that the more successful my cooperative is the more antagonism it will arouse. From time immemorial it has been taken for granted that the producer must remain poor and those who market his products grow rich. Cooperatives are organized so that the producer may enter the market place himself.

I know that organizations such as newspapers, banks, power companies, and grocery stores have nonprofit organizations to assist them in doing business, and I claim the same right. Having created, along with my neighbors, an organization to assist in the production and marketing of my crops, I cannot sell on the side. I must stand by my convictions and be faithful to them. I must be as honest with my cooperative as I expect it to be with me.

A loyal cooperator helps his organization serve its members; he combats divisions in the ranks; he knows the danger of competing cooperatives fighting for the loyalties of the community.[14] The very word "cooperative" means working together.

[14]*Joseph G. Knapp, "Cooperative Destiny—It's Up to You,"* Cooperative Digest *(March 1963), 4.*

2. Am I Informed?

Jose Rizal, the great leader of Philippine independence, said: "As liberty is to men, so is education to intellect." To be a member of a cooperative I must know the fundamentals of cooperation. I must be familiar with the business of which I am a part. When I chose to sell my crops to the wholesaler and to purchase my supplies from the retailer, I had no obligation to study the markets. I bought and sold on a day-by-day basis; if I made a mistake no one but myself and my family was hurt. Now that I have become a member of a joint effort I must be acquainted with the needs of my cooperative so that my judgments may be of value to the membership.

Cooperatives, despite their nonprofit character, are business ventures with all the problems of other businesses. My responsibility to my cooperative is not fulfilled when I cast my vote for the directors I prefer. I still have the obligation to keep informed on how my cooperative is functioning.

3. Am I Communicative?

When I was in business for myself, I was a lone wolf. Now that I have become a member of a mutual society, I have the obligation to communicate to my fellow-producers the things that I have learned about our cooperative.

If I leave all membership solicitation to the manager and his staff, I am not making my personal contribution to the cooperative. I should not debate with noncooperators, but rather give them the facts about cooperation. I should point out my reasons for being a member.

4. Am I alert?

I can learn much from the Biblical story of Gideon. You will remember how Gideon and his ten thousand men arrived at a stream after a long march. Most of the warriors dropped to their stomach and lapped up the water like dogs. Three hundred of them, however, remained alert, their weapons held ready for the enemy, and drank with restraint, erect on one knee, drinking with their weaponless hand. These were the three hundred Gideon chose for his mission. So must I, like Gideon's elite troops, be ever on guard and prepared to warn my cooperative of danger. I know that there are those who would like to destroy our cooperative because they wish to keep the mass of human beings as peons. I do not hate these profiteers, but I take precautions against them. I live under a free government. I do not have to give what I produce to others to market. My fellow-members and I have chosen to market our produce through our cooperative. Our decision must guide my conduct.

5. Am I a Permanent Member?

When I married, I did so for life, and I did not contemplate eventual divorce. The loyal cooperator behaves similarly. He has chosen to join with his neighbors in a common cause. He is defeating the very purpose of the organization if he does not accept membership unreservedly. The curse of in-and-out membership is perhaps the greatest single reason why cooperatives fail. If I find that there are things about the cooperative that I do not like, it must be my duty either to change them or learn to live with them. I must not desert the cause because of a few mistakes made by management or my fellow-members. Perhaps, upon closer examination, I will find that I myself am responsible in part for the very things that dissatisfy me.

6. Am I an Independent Member?

Many cooperatives have been wrecked because members insist on government help. But the very theory of cooperation implies self-help. The government has done its part by providing statutes which make the organization possible. Many cooperators have not informed themselves of the dangers of government control.

As government performs increasing services for the cooperative, the benefits of cooperative action decrease in direct proportion. In the Soviet world there are organizations also called "cooperatives," but which are, in fact, the direct antithesis of true cooperation. Mine is a group of free people who have voluntarily decided to perform services for themselves. In the Soviet "cooperative," the farmers are compelled to join the organization and the officers are responsible not to the membership but to the political overlords. This is compulsion, not cooperation. While we have no immediate threat of such practices in our country, we must not forget that inevitably increased participation by government will bring increased control.

There is nothing more representative of the people than a democratically operated cooperative whose goal is economic freedom within the framework of political freedom. If cooperatives perform their work intelligently and efficiently, there should be less and less need for governmental aid to farmers. I recommend that members try to make their cooperative function without governmental subsidies. People lose their independence, their integrity, and their autonomy when they depend upon the government.

7. Am I a Producer?

To be a member of a farmer cooperative association presupposes that I am an efficient farmer. If I am slovenly in my work, if I abuse the soil rather than tend it, I am defeating not only my own chance of success but that of my neighbors and my children. I must try to farm so that my land will produce abundant crops on a "sustained yield" basis. My cooperative cannot perform a miracle and present good salable products to the consumer if the product I produce is not of high quality. If my cooperative is to be a vital, permanent organization, its customers must be kept satisfied.

8. Am I a Businessman?

The world often considers farmers as unable to succeed in more significant ventures. Cooperatives are helping to change

126

this pernicious belief. Those of us who are members of cooperatives now are able to say:

> I have chosen to be a business partner with my neighbors. My cooperative has made it possible for me to own many things that I could not before. I operate my crop land with more and better tools than did my father. My house has more conveniences than did the house of my parents. My children go to better schools than I did. Together with my fellows, I have built a better community than we had before the cooperative began to function. All of these changes are the results of my family's business judgment pooled with that of my neighbors. What we have accomplished is only the beginning of what will happen in the years to come.

Cooperatives must recognize that life is based on change. The farmer of 1825 used essentially the same tools as his ancestors and achieved no greater harvest than did his ancestors. If we are to move forward, we cannot be bound to the tools or techniques of even twenty years ago. The techniques for marketing and producing have changed. Remember that the warehouses and processing plants of the world were paid for by the profits from handling farm products—the big difference between these non-cooperative plants and those of a cooperative organization is that the cooperative member owns his jointly with his neighbors.

Cooperatives must serve their members with all their vocational needs. Cooperatives, when they help members to purchase equipment for production, assist the economy by promoting solvency. Farmers the world over have generally been poor. Why? Because they buy at retail and sell at wholesale. The cooperative, when it functions properly, puts an end to this inequity.

I must realize that I have become a businessman-farmer, and need take off my hat to no man. My occupation is as important as any other. I must learn how to keep my books, conserve my machinery and land, save for the future, in short, do

127

all those things that were formerly thought to be only the province of the economic entrepreneur. I can and will work with my neighbors so that our properties will become more and more valuable.

9. Do I Have a Family Membership?

Have I learned that my wife and children are my partners? They profit when I prosper and they suffer when I make mistakes. Cooperatives the world over have succeeded in proportion to the degree to which women are allowed to participate in them. Cooperation is really a magnification of the family circle. When the wives, mothers, and children are an active part of the "cooperative thinking," then we have utilized the intellect of all. We can learn much from our enemies, and one thing the Soviets have taught is not to underestimate the judgment of women and the young. Cooperation cannot survive in times of stress unless all members of the family are loyal to it. The cooperative is a new type of corporation; one of its great strengths is that its decisions are not by the few, but by the many.

10. Am I Understanding?

In 1947, I wrote a little Public Relations book entitled "Take Time for Human Engineering."[15] In it I said:

> There are twelve essential principles upon which the art and science of constructive human engineering are based. Each is important. To overlook any one is as fatal to the end result as for a structural engineer to forget to calculate stresses, a highway engineer to neglect gradients and curves, or a physician to fail by etiology to find the complete syndrome. It makes little difference whether a person be a social or mechanical engineer, a professional man, a farmer, a businessman, or a government employee; the basic principles of human engineering are involved in the group activities of each. These may be ex-

[15]Published by World Trade Relations, Inc., Dupont Circle Building, Washington, D.C.

pressed in twelve words:

1. Alertness
2. Energy
3. Planning
4. Research
5. Judgment
6. Humility
7. Sacrifice
8. Faith
9. Sincerity
10. Service
11. Honesty
12. Understanding

The next-to-last draft of this manuscript had "toleration" rather than "understanding" as the twelfth item.

I sent a prepublication copy to my good friend, Alcuin Deutsch, the late Abbott of St. John's Abbey at Collegeville, Minnesota. He returned it to me with the comment:

> Raymond, you don't mean "toleration," you mean "understanding." To tolerate is merely to recognize as being in existence, but not to appreciate. When we try to understand our neighbor or our critic or our avowed enemy, we are God-minded; to merely tolerate is man-minded.

Nowhere is this divine trait of understanding needed more than in cooperatives. As we build for ourselves and our neighbors, let us also try to understand those who have not as yet "seen the faith" of mutual work. As we try to understand them, we may ourselves be understood.

When Shakespeare wrote: "To thine own self be true, and, it must follow as the night the day, thou canst not then be false to any man," he prescribed the infallible formula for human happiness and for cooperative success.

When Jesus Christ said, "As a man thinketh in his heart so is he," he spelled out the perfect measurement of life for all men and for those in particular who have chosen to be members of a cooperative.

If when we joined our cooperative we did so for purely selfish reasons, the cooperative will fail because *we willed* it to. If we joined wanting it to succeed, *it will succeed*.

Cooperatives must succeed because they are one of the essentials of democracy. Only the membership of cooperatives can make them succeed. Let's keep our particular vertebra of "Economic Democracy" functioning smoothly in its place as a part of the backbone of democracy.

VI. Legal Basis of Cooperatives and Other Nonprofit Corporations

"There is no legal objection to persons organizing a corporation to effect savings for its members or stockholders."

"Farm people, agricultural producers, may get together as a group of individuals to form, own, and manage a nonprofit cooperative, whether unincorporated or incorporated, to market their products. In so doing they have the right to organize without violating antitrust legislation."

"The nonprofit corporation is used by many forms of individually owned businesses, ranging from individual grocers purchasing jointly, to power companies mutually purchasing transformers, to newspapers gathering news, such as the Associated Press. Individual consumers often use the same type cooperative corporate entity for the purchase of insurance, hospitals, apartments, and an occasional grocery store."

COOPERATIVES AND THE LAW

As a long-time member of the Bar and as an acquaintance, friend, or associate of attorneys, barristers, solicitors, jurists, and advocates in two-score countries, I have, through observation and discussion, come to some basic conclusions about cooperatives and the law, which I should like to present here.[1]

[1] *These thoughts were first expressed by Raymond W. Miller at the annual meeting of the Linden Walnut Growers Association, Linden, California, April 9, 1962.*

A Conservative Looks At Cooperatives

Courts Are Basically the Custodians of the Liberties of a Free People

There is much misunderstanding about the place of the judiciary in the Free World. Basically the courts are the interpreters of actions of natural and artificial persons when these actions have been challenged by another person in a civil action or by the state in a criminal prosecution.

If the layman will look upon the court of last resort or final determination as being basically the custodian of the liberties of a free people, he will have a fundamental understanding of the purposes of the judiciary. Courts try to arrive at the facts and adjudicate upon them under law, even though these facts may be obscured by poor observation, poor memory, poor records, the shadows of time, or even fraud itself.

Recently I had occasion to be with the Chief Justice of the United States, Mr. Justice Warren, together with Mrs. Emerson Hynes of Arlington, Virginia. Mrs. Hynes, although not an attorney, has for many years closely observed the workings of the Supreme Court of the United States. In conversation, she told Mr. Warren that she had listened to literally hundreds of cases before the Supreme Court, ranging from actions in regard to transportation rates to those involving the most violent of major crimes. She said she had come to a basic conclusion: namely, that the questions of the members of the court, as they interrogated attorneys, all fell into two categories: What is the truth? and, What effect will this case have on the liberties of a free people?

Nonprofit Corporation Pays Taxes Same As Profit Corporation

With this observation on the functions of the judiciary, let's now look at the nonprofit corporation and the law.[2] Basically,

[2]*One of the most illuminating statements of the place of the nonprofit corporation in the economy was presented at a*

132

the cooperative pays the same general property, sales, and municipal taxes as any other corporation. If it erects a building, it pays the same tax on that improvement as the profit and loss corporation would if it owned the building. If it hires employees, it pays the same social security, workmen's compensation and unemployment taxes as a private business.

Thousands of Cooperatives Pay Income Taxes; Public Led to Misunderstand the Situation

When it comes to determining corporate income and taxes thereon the cooperative unjustly is vilified. There have been more articles, more vilification, more misinformation, and more misunderstanding about the cooperative's alleged "escape" from, or avoidance of, income taxes than there has been in regard to any other current business question.

Except for statutory deductions on dividends and income from nonpatronage sources, all nonprofit cooperatives are subject to federal and state income tax laws.[3] If a cooperative

meeting in San Francisco, August 7, 1945, by Dr. E. A. Stokdyk under the title "Public Interest in the Cooperative Controversy." This historic study is presented in full in Joseph G. Knapp's STOKDYK—ARCHITECT OF COOPERATION *(Washington, D.C., 1953), p. 207 ff.*

Ernest L. Wilkinson, one of America's leading corporation lawyers and President of Brigham Young University, Provo, Utah, made a landmark presentation at Utah State University in 1951 entitled "Cooperative Business in Our Economy." Among other things he said that marketing cooperatives are capitalistic because they exist to make money for their owners. The whole paper is worthy of careful study. See AMERICAN COOPERATION, *1951 (American Institute of Cooperation, Washington, D.C.), p. 44.*

[3] *L. S. Hulbert, revised and extended by Raymond J. Mischler,* LEGAL PHASES OF FARMER COOPERATIVES, *Farmer Cooperative Service, FCS Bulletin 10, United States Department of Agriculture (Washington, D.C., January, 1958). A highly authoritative, well-documented legal treatise covering this field.*

makes a profit, it pays an income tax. It is true that about half of the 10,000 farmer cooperatives qualify for what is called tax exempt status. The only advantage approved by some federal courts for agricultural cooperatives prior to the Revenue Act of October 20, 1951, was to exclude dividends paid on stock, if any, and income, if any, realized from non-patronage business, such as profits from sales of real property, rents, interest and earnings on investments. After the passing of this Act, mandatory patronage refunds, which the courts had repeatedly held earlier were to be "excluded" were declared to be deductible from the income of an agricultural cooperative complying with the requirements of the Revenue Act of 1951, Sections 521 and 522. One of the new requirements of this Act was that net proceeds must be allocated to patrons within 8½ months after the close of each fiscal year.

If a "cooperative" actually operates as a cooperative, it can make little or no profit. True nonexempt cooperatives agree to operate at cost for the benefit of their patrons and thus have no income on business done for or with patrons and none or little non-patronage income which is then taxable.

Basically, if a nonprofit corporation keeps within the purposes for which it was established and serves its members at cost, it has no patronage income of its own. It acts as an agent or agency or servant for its patron members (sometimes in a very literal sense—sometimes in a very broad nontechnical sense): it agrees to perform a service or handle money and goods for them at cost. Incidentally, any profit and loss corporation can do the same thing if it wants to make a prior contract with its patrons to operate at cost. (The Ford Motor Company did this to a limited degree by making an agreed cash refund to an amount of fifteen million dollars to purchasers of the Model T cars for the year of 1914-1915.)

Use of Proper Terms Would Greatly Reduce Public Confusion

Unfortunately, cooperatives have often been represented by officers, members, attorneys, and auditors who have become confused in terminology, who have not taken the time to learn the basic differences in purpose and method of operation between a profit and a nonprofit business corporation.

For instance, when a cooperative announces that it is paying a "dividend," any intelligent person assumes that the cooperative is a profit organization and should pay an income tax. If the cooperative will use good, honest language and speak of the mandatory returns on its overcharge for services as a patronage refund or reimbursement rather than as a dividend, it will save itself from being misunderstood. Patronage dividend is a phrase that may be accurately used to characterize nonpatronage income distributed on a patronage basis rather than proportionally to investment.

It is interesting to note that the high courts have universally recognized that when the cooperative acts in effect as an agent under a prior contract to refund overcharges, it has no problem in regard to the income tax on funds temporarily received but promptly paid in cash or cash equivalent to its patrons. This is true even though the patron supplies his patronage refund to his cooperative as some form of invested corporate capital or loan for capital purposes.

There is much misunderstanding about the patronage refund of consumer cooperatives. The money that is paid into a cooperatively run grocery store by a patron is not usually considered a business expense, but a series of personal expense transactions producing saving upon an accounting by the cooperative to each of its patrons. Consequently, any refund that comes to the recipient is not taxable, because it merely is a mandatory refund of a saving to the patron by the cooperative. If the refund is on a previous business charge, other than the purchase of business equipment or fixtures which are depreciable annually, then it is taxable to the patron if he has deducted the cost of the original business purchase in a prior income tax return.

British Legal Decision of Great Importance in Establishing Cooperative Status

A number of legal decisions have done much to clarify the status of nonprofit corporations. None is more significant than the decision made by the British House of Lords in the case of New York Life Insurance Company v. Styles (Surveyor of Taxes).[4] The following is a summary of the case.

The life insurance company had no shares or shareholders. The only members were the holders of participating policies, each of whom was entitled to a share of the assets and liable for losses. A calculation was made by the company of the probable death rate among the members and of the probable expenses and other liabilities, and the amount received for premiums from members was commensurate therewith. An account was annually taken and the greater part of the surplus of such premiums over expenditures referable to these policies was returned to the policyholders, either by addition to the sums insured or in reduction of future premiums. The remainder of the surplus was carried forward as funds in hand to the credit of the general body of the members, it being admitted that the income *derived* by the company from investments and from all transactions with persons not members was assessable to income tax as corporate income.

The court held that no part of the premium income received under participating policies was liable to be assessed to income tax as profits or gains.

The court really decided this case on the ground that it was an instance merely of mutual insurance, similar to a situ-

[4]*British Law Reports, 14 Appeal Cases 381 (1889).*

ation where several persons contribute sums toward a book club, to continue for a year. At the end of the year the expenses are less than the fund. The amounts returned are not profits. The contributors cannot make a profit from themselves; therefore, the sums returned are merely savings over estimates of cost.

Canadian Decision Confirms Principle of No Profit Earned by a True Mutual Business

Another important decision was handed down by the Supreme Court of Canada and concerned an action brought by the Minister of National Revenue against the Stanley Mutual Fire Insurance Company.[5]

The Stanley Mutual Fire Insurance Company was incorporated as a provincial mutual company under the New Brunswick Companies Act, as amended in 1937, to undertake contracts of insurance against loss by fire and other specified causes upon farm and other non-hazardous property under the premium note plan subject to certain provisions of an applicable Insurance Act. Insurance was issued upon premium notes upon which a cash payment was secured prior to the issuance of the policy and the notes were subject to further assessments to meet losses and expense incurred during the term of the policy. Where this annual amount collected in cash exceeded the current year's losses and expenses, the surplus became part of the reserves fund. In 1947, the Company transferred (as provided by the Act) a surplus of $6,103.60 to its reserve fund. This amount was assessed under the income tax as taxable income, constituting an annual net profit or gain.

It was the court's opinion that the reserve funds were accumulated as directed by the Act of 1937, not in pursuance of a profit-making enterprise but in furtherance of a mutual insurance plan carried on by the Company in the interest of its members to provide a statutory actuarial fund. The fund

[5] *1953 Canada Law Reports 442.*

could not be applied (except on order of the Governor in Council) to any purpose other than the settlement of claims or other liabilities. On a winding-up, the surplus, if any, under the provisions of the Winding-Up Act of 1927 and the Insurance Act of 1937, read together, would be returned to the members of the company. The moneys so accumulated were held not to be income within the meaning of the income tax laws.

The broad principle was laid down that, if the interest in the money does not go beyond the people or the class of people who subscribed it, then just as there is no profit earned by the people subscribing, if they do the thing for themselves, so there is none if they get a company to do it for them. The New York Life Insurance Company vs. Styles, *supra*, was cited to support this decision.

U. S. Court Upholds Nonprofit Service Corporation in Railroad Bridge Case

Cases in the United States have followed this same legal thinking. One of the most significant of these is the Appeal of Paducah and Illinois Railroad Company.[6]

Three railroads had incorporated a nonprofit company to build and operate a bridge for transportation of railroad rolling stock at cost. By contract each railroad was to pay established rates to the nonprofit service corporation based upon its use of the bridge. At the end of the year any overage was to be returned to the railroads in preferred stock on a patronage basis.

At the accounting period it was found that there was a sizeable overcharge to be refunded in stock of the nonprofit corporation to the participating railroads as a means of supplying stock capital to the bridge cooperative to liquidate a bond issue utilized to pay the initial costs of building the bridge.

The income tax officials considered the amount received

[6] *Board of Tax Appeals 1001 (1925)*.

138

as capital on the continuing stock subscription of the members a profit to the bridge corporation and as such subject to income tax assessment. The bridge company appealed the levy on the ground that the corporation was merely a nonprofit (cooperative) service agency for the participating railroad members.

The court granted the petitioners' plea and rendered a decision in line with the legal thinking of the two cases cited above—one from the United Kingdom and the other from the Crowned Democracy of Canada.

These basic decisions from Britain, Canada, and the United States agreed on the basic principles that a nonprofit corporation when acting within the scope of its charter is an agency for its member patrons. These rulings are still good interpretive law and will continue to be so for as long as courts adjudicate within the framework of the common law.[7]

Reductio ad absurdum—Should Boy Scouts Pay Tax on $15.50 Refund?

A short newspaper item from the Memphis, Tennessee, *Commercial Appeal,* of February 5, 1958, reads as follows:

Scouts to Get Refund
    Philadelphia, Feb. 4. The 50,000 Boy Scouts and

[7]*Decisions from the highest courts in non-common law jurisdiction in the Free World interpret the powers and actions of nonprofit corporations in a similar fashion.*

Irwin Clawson, one of the most knowledgeable corporation attorneys in the western United States, in a paper called "Recent Cooperative Cases" presented at the Utah State University in 1951, draws attention to the fact that money handled for patron members by a cooperative is really a trust fund. He cites two leading cases in this document which I, as a fellow member of the Bar, recommend for careful reading; i.e., Broadcast Measurement Bureau v. Commissioner, 16 TC 122; and Chicago, Milwaukee & St. Paul Railway Co. et al., v. Des Moines Union Railroad Co., et al., 254, U. S. 196.

> their leaders who paid a $50 registration fee to attend
> the fourth national Boy Scout jamboree at Valley Forge,
> Penn., last July are each going to get a $15.50 refund.
> Dr. Pliny H. Powers, deputy chief Scout executive, said
> the refund, totalling about $800,000, results from careful
> management of jamboree expenses.

Should the Boy Scouts of America pay a tax on the $800,-
000? Should the individual Boy Scout members pay a tax on
the $15.50? In the answer to those questions lies the whole
basis for not taxing as profit the mandatory return made by a
nonprofit business organization of an overcharge or of a deferred payment by a marketing cooperative.

Committee of American Bar Association Clarifies Legal Background of Cooperatives

In the mid-40's, the American Bar Association became
interested in the development of law affecting a "new kind of
critter"—the cooperative.[8] It authorized its president to appoint a special committee to deal with the problem of clari-
fication and legal terminology of the nonprofit cooperative corporation.

This committee was chaired by Dr. A. Ladru Jensen,
Professor of Corporation Law of the University of Utah, and
also my associate as General Counsel of the American Institute
of Cooperation. The report of the Jensen Committee is a legal
landmark and was printed in full in the *Business Lawyer*,
November 17, 1949, and in the *Proceedings of the American
Bar Association*, 1949.

> In my opinion, we are on the threshold of a great-
> er development of cooperative corporation law. What the
> turn will be, I am unable to predict. There is, however,
> or should be a real thrill for every lawyer who is helping

[8]*Eugene L. Hensel, "Taxation of Cooperatives," in A. Ladru
Jensen et al, COOPERATIVE CORPORATE ASSOCIATION LAW
(American Institute of Cooperation, Washington, D.C., 1950),
p. 70.*

mold a body of law in its initial stages. It will be many and many a year before the cooperative corporation as a *sui generis* will be recognized and accepted by the bar generally, but, that result I think I can safely predict. It seems inevitable. There is no one branch of the law of business, be it agency or corporation, partnership or trust which fully embraces and satisfies all the wants and necessities of a cooperative. It is by the blending and admixture of all four of these branches of law, aided, and abetted by the law of contract, that the characteristics of this *sui generis* business unit will be determined. As Congressman Martin of Iowa stated: "It is beginning to dawn on me that we have a *new kind of critter.*"

This report, together with several others was later incorporated in a volume assembled by Dr. Jensen.[9] In that volume, Dr. Jensen says:

> Within the last five years the United States Supreme Court has recognized and declared the Associated Press with over 1200 private-profit newspaper member-patrons to be a nonprofit cooperative corporation. Only last year the Circuit Court of Appeals of The Second Circuit held that the Railway Express Agency was incorporated as a nonprofit cooperative association having about 70 railroad companies as its profit seeking patron-members.[10]

[9]COOPERATIVE CORPORATE ASSOCIATION LAW, *p. 70. See also Raymond W. Miller and Herbert R. Grossman, "The Non-profit Corporation or Association in the Nonagricultural Field,"* LAW AND CONTEMPORARY PROBLEMS, *XIII (1948), 465-466, citing among other cases, Associated Press v. United States, 326 U.S. 1, 89 L Ed. 2013 (1945).*

[10]*Railway Express Agency v. Commissioner of Internal Revenue, 169 F. 2d. 193 (1948) affirming 8 T.C. 991:*

> *The court also held that the Railway Express Agency had not operated "at cost" because it had accumulated depreciation reserves substantially in excess of actual economic depreciation of its properties. Such excess was held to be profits in the hands of corporation, originally intended to be incorporated as a nonprofit cooperative corporation.*

Dr. Jensen goes on (p. 71) to say:

Examination of the Agricultural Cooperative Association Acts of the forty-eight states discloses that they all declare the non-profit nature of the cooperative corporation, while also declaring the purpose to make profits for its producer members. Such study also discloses the use by many statutes of the inconsistent terms: "earnings," "income" and "surplus" of the association declared to be a nonprofit entity.

This evident inconsistency has necessitated many decisions by state supreme courts and the federal courts, including the Tax Court, to determine from time to time whether the particular cooperative corporate association was legally a nonprofit agent or trustee,[11] of its corporate members, or whether it did have some "corporate income," or "earnings" on business which should have been done by it solely as a nonprofit agent for the "mutual benefit" of its member patrons, except as dividends might be paid on capital stock.

Income Tax Status of Capital Derived from Refund

There is much confusion in the minds of students of the law, cooperative managers, and directors in regard to the assembly of reserves. This subject is adequately covered in *Cooperative Corporate Association Law, supra,* but, basically, it is well to remember that the court decisions recognize that the member patron of a nonprofit service organization may elect by

---

[11]*The California Appellate Court declared in Bogardus v. Santa Ana Walnut Growers Ass'n, 41 Cal. App. 2d 939, 108 P. 2d 52 (1940), "At all times the relationship between the grower member and the local association, and between the local association and the central association, was that of principal and agent, or beneficiary and trustee; that a fiduciary relationship existed which required at all times that these associations account to the grower member for all proceeds received from the sale of walnuts, and required the grower to bear its proportionate share of all losses sustained." Jensen, Id. at 534.*

contract with the cooperative to invest any part or all of his savings in the capital structure of the cooperative. He, the patron investor, should pay an income tax or not upon this amount, depending upon its source. If the sum in question is merely a contribution or loan of capital (coming from an allocation of a refund of overpayment) to a consumer cooperative for items for personal or family uses, then it is not subject to income tax either to the cooperative or to the patron.

If it represents deferred income to the individual because of the services rendered by his cooperative in selling of his farm products, then the amount should be taxed to the patron. Also, if it represents a refund of an overpayment to a vocational supply cooperative for an item which affects a patron's business income (and is not a depreciable capital item), it should be currently taxable to the patron. So long as the cooperative is an agent for its patrons and receives net patronage margins under a preexisting obligation of debt to its patrons, the cooperative is not liable to income tax thereon.[12] Corporations are not taxable on monies paid on debts whether paid in cash or cash equivalent.

The United States Revenue Act of 1962, enacted October 16, 1962, reaffirms the principle of collecting only a single tax on income generated through a nonprofit corporate association such as a farmer marketing and purchasing cooperative. It provides that net proceeds of sales and savings when allocated and noticed to patrons within a specified time may be taxed singly to patrons who consent to take patronage distributions into their account as income on a partnership basis. The exceptions are personal or family items in which overcharges by the coop-

[12]*In order to be a true cooperative, however, the decisions emphasize that there must be a legal obligation on the part of the association, made before the receipt of income, to return to the members on a patronage basis all funds received in excess of cost of goods sold. Such an obligation may arise from the association's articles of incorporation, its bylaws, or some other contract. American Box Shook Export Co. v. C.I.R., 156 F. 2d 629 (9 Cir. 1946).*

erative and mandatory patronage refunds are not taxable income to either cooperative or patron. Other cooperatives (such as organizations performing buying or other services for their members) are accorded like treatment.

These cooperatives are to be permitted to reduce their alleged gross income for federal income tax purposes to the extent of patronage refunds (erroneously called "patronage dividends" in the law) paid to the patrons in cash or by allocations if the patron has the option to redeem the allocations in cash during a 90-day period after issuance, or consents in various ways stated in the Act to treating this income as constructively received and reinvested in or loaned to the cooperative for capital purposes. The patron may give his consent individually in writing, or the cooperative may by its bylaws cause members to give their consent, or patrons may give their consent by endorsing a check representing at least 20 per cent of the total "patronage dividend." For any allocation to be deductible to the cooperative, however, at least 20 per cent of the so-called "patronage dividend" (mainly a patronage refund) must be paid in cash.

Any of these amounts which are deductible to the cooperative must be included in the income of the patron for tax purposes when received if the amounts arise from business activity of the patron. However, inclusion is not necessary if the refund covers the cost of equipment which is depreciable annually; in such a case the amount is not includable in the patron's income but merely reduces the cost of the item on which depreciation will be allowed.

Courts Have Favored Joint Action Through Purchasing or Service Cooperatives

Another phase of cooperative activity that is not understood as well as it should be is the relation of cooperatives to antitrust legislation. Fortunately, the Supreme Court of the United

States has very adequately settled the status of the incorporated cooperative association, as well as what it may do in the field of marketing products.[13]

A purchasing cooperative, or other nonmarketing service cooperative, that performs with integrity work for its members has in general little to fear from antitrust laws. The decisions of the courts have invariably favored people joining together to purchase collectively. This is in the interests of the consumer as a purchaser. There is no legal objection to persons organizing a corporation to effect savings for its members or stockholders.

However, when it came to the matter of farm people gathering together in order to sell their products cooperatively to secure a fairer price, the individual farmers immediately ran afoul of the law forbidding combinations in restraint of trade. A number of Pennsylvania milk farmers were actually arrested in the early part of this century. The farmers' "crime" was that they had joined together with their neighbors to market milk and other products cooperatively in order to gain a better price in an oversupplied market. Under the provisions of the various antitrust laws in the United States and the common law of Britain, early efforts of such farmers to compete more favorably by joint action in the marketing of their products were not within the scope of permissive legal action.

Individual Farmers Recognized to Have Right to Organize to Market Cooperatively

However, public policy in all the Free World has since recognized that individual farmers will become a depressed economic group if left to the mercy of large purchasing groups and profit-seeking middlemen. All free governments recognize that the individual farmer is a mainstay of democracy. Laws that would stop farm people from getting together to help

[13]*U. S. v. Maryland and Virginia Milk Producers Association 362 U. S. 458 1960.*

themselves would be contrary to the farmers' interest, which in a substantial degree is also the public interest. So there have been statutes passed in all of the states of the United States and by the Congress granting farmers the right to get together to form organizations to collectively market their products and buy their equipment and supplies.[14] Similar enactments are practically universal throughout the Free World.

Farm people, agricultural producers, may get together as a group of individuals to form, own, and manage a nonprofit cooperative, whether unincorporated or incorporated, to market their products. In so doing they have the right to organize without violating antitrust legislation. This exemption has been necessary for farmers because similar combinations of middlemen to enhance price are injurious to the public interest and are still restrained by law.[15]

[14]*The Capper-Volstead Act, 42 Stat. 388 (1922) 7 U.S.C.A. Sec. 291 (1940)*

[15]*Among the citations showing how the courts restrain agreements as to supply and demand, and arrangements as to selective markets the following is typical:*

United States v. Jellico Mountain Coal & Coke Co., 46 Fed. 432 (1891)

"The petition in this case is filed against the members of the Nashville Coal Exchange. The membership of the exchange is composed of various coal mining companies operating mines in Kentucky and Tennessee, chiefly in Kentucky, and the persons and firms dealing in coal at Nashville, Tenn.

"The articles of agreement between the defendants provide, among other things, that the objects of this exchange are 'To do all in its power to advance the interests of the coal business in Nashville, to treat all parties to this agreement in a fair and equitable manner, and to establish prices on coal at Nashville, Tenn., and to change same from time to time, as occasion may require.'

"Coal classed as No. 1 shall be valued at the mines at 4½ cents minimum price for 80 pounds lump, and freight being 4 cents, the dealers margin to be 4½ cents, making the price of lump coal 13 cents per bushel.

Even without exempting legislation, however, the courts of the United States began to recognize the overwhelming public opinion of the 1920's that the normal operations of farmer cooperatives were not in unreasonable restraint of trade. Although the enabling federal legislation in this field was all enacted prior to 1930, there was only limited litigation producing judicial interpretations of the existing laws[16] until the decision of the United States Supreme Court in the case of Maryland and Virginia Milk Producers Association on May 2, 1960, clarified this exemption.[17]

The Supreme Court declared that when the cooperative has been formed, it, the cooperative, is then looked upon by the law as any other corporation. It must abide by the rules of fair play; it must abide by the provisions of the antitrust and

> "*Any member of the exchange who may withdraw from it, and continue in the coal trade shall forfeit and relinquish all interest of any and every kind, however obtained or accrued.*
>
> "*The question is whether the agreement and regulations between the defendants are a 'contract or combination in restraint of trade or commerce between states.'*
>
> "*Held, The exchange does not propose to be governed and controlled by the public markets arising from competition and the operations of the laws of supply and demand. On the contrary, it announces that its purpose is 'to establish prices on coal at Nashville, Tenn., and to change the same from time to time as occasion may require.'*
>
> "*The restraint is positive and undeniable.*
>
> "*I conclude that the defendants by the organization of the Nashville Coal Exchange, and their operation under it, have been, and at the time of filing the petition in this cause were, guilty of a violation of Sections 1 and 2 of the Act of July 2, 1890, and should be enjoined from further violation of the law, as provided in the fourth section thereof.*"
>
> [16]*See John Hanna, "Antitrust Immunities of Cooperative Associations,"* Law and Contemporary Problems, XIII *(Summer 1948), 488-504.*
>
> [17]*362 U.S. 458.*

anticartel legislation. It may not engage in predatory practices, combine with other corporations to raise prices, or under the Kefauver Act[18] acquire the assets of a competitor in such a way as to substantially lessen competition.

Cooperatives Must Operate in Conformity With Antitrust Laws

If the managers of farmer-owned cooperatives will recognize that in their operation as managers of the corporate entity they must act in regard to the laws exactly as though they were directing any commercial corporation, then they should have no trouble with the antitrust laws. If, however, they act upon the assumption that the cooperative is entitled to exemptions from the antitrust laws not accorded to other corporations, then the government has a perfect right to step in.

In summary, farm people are free to organize a cooperative to market their products. Once the cooperative has been formed, it must operate under the rules which are applicable to any other corporation and it must gain its new members without engaging in unfair competition.

Anyone interested in pursuing this matter further should read the decision of the Supreme Court in the Maryland and Virginia Milk Producers Association case, *supra,* and the exposition of this case printed in the proceedings of the American Institute of Cooperation, *American Cooperation,* 1960.[19] These statements are broad in their scope, factual in their understand-

[18]*Amendment to the Clayton Act of 1914, on December 29, 1950, 15 U.S.C.A. Sec. 18.*
[19]*Donald D. Stark, "Capper-Volstead Revisited: An Analysis of the Supreme Court Decision in U.S. v. Maryland and Virginia Milk Producers Association, Inc.,"* American Cooperation, *1960, p. 453 ff.; Raymond J. Mischler, "Current Legal Developments Affecting Farmer Cooperatives,"* American Cooperation, *1960, p. 474 ff.; and Sherman R. Hill, "Agricultural Cooperatives and the Federal Trade Commission,"* American Cooperation, *1960, p. 443 ff.*

ing, and accurate in their conclusions.

Freedom from antitrust prosecution has helped make the nonprofit marketing corporation one of the bulwarks of freedom.

Various Types of Business Enterprise Active in a Free Economy

A capitalistic economy such as we have developed in the United States expresses itself in various types of private enterprise. The government operates various forms of business. These range from some 2,000 municipal electric systems to a cement mill in South Dakota owned by the state. All of these enterprises are "socialistic" as defined by the classical socialists and are, in the main, in direct competition with private business.

Under our form of popular government, however, ownership and/or operation of such enterprises often shifts from the state to private hands and vice versa. Recently the city of New York divested itself of a giant electric utility which then became part of a private power company. In the Midwest, states and municipalities have from time to time operated grain elevators which have been later sold to private entrepreneurs. Farmer cooperatives have acquired facilities and personnel of the private-profit grain companies. Also some cooperatives have sold to private profit corporations. Often by vote of the people or legislative action a private enterprise is expropriated by the state and recompense as determined by the court is given to the original owners. In other words, we have a mixed economy and all political parties in North America recognize that this is what we as a free people want.[20]

Businesses

One inequity which often causes great distress when the

[20]*See Harold Koontz and Richard W. Gable,* PUBLIC CONTROL OF ECONOMIC ENTERPRISE *(New York, 1956), p. 19.*

state takes over some enterprise relates to taxation; the state pays no tax on the businesses it operates. There is a recent trend toward equalization of tax payments by government-owned utilities: in the case of the Tennessee Valley Authority the government does make an agreed payment in lieu of taxes. However, government as a rule does not take over unless private business fails to give adequate service at fair prices, or unless, as in the case of the Alaskan Railway and the REA cooperatives, private capital has left the job undone.

Income Tax Payments Required on Profits, But Cooperatives As Agencies Make No Profits Themselves

Private business falls into various categories. Individual owners and operators, such as farmers, storekeepers, truckers, and specialty shops operated by an individual, pay property taxes upon their holdings and a personal income tax upon their profits.

Partnerships, of which there are millions, operate as individual owners in paying property taxes but pay no income tax—the profits are divided among the partners according to their respective interests and income tax on them is paid by the individual and not the partnership even though the firm retains its profits to expand the business.

Incorporated Business Falls into Two Similar Areas

The profit and loss corporation, which is the great majority of all corporate business, pays property taxes upon its holdings and also pays a corporate income tax if it has net earnings. Its profits, after the payment to the government of its share, are retained in part to expand the business and paid in part to its stockholders, as dividends upon capital. Stockholders, in turn, pay individual income taxes upon their returns. Thus, in the U.S., there is a double taxation upon corporate dividends except for the present $50 exemption to each person.

The true nonprofit corporation or incorporated partnership acts as an agent or agency for its members because it makes no profit on patronage transactions and thus is not liable to income tax. This cooperative corporate form of business appeals to an increasing number of different types of business because it enables the members of the cooperative entity to compete more effectively with larger corporate businesses. It has as its legal objective the preservation of the individual businesses of the members who use the nonprofit cooperative corporation as a business tool for their joint activities. There is increasing friction with the profit and loss corporations which have earnings and therefore income taxes on those earnings.

What is not generally known is that the National Council of Farmer Cooperatives, the American Farm Bureau Federation, and the National Grange in the mid-forties passed strong resolutions petitioning Congress to eliminate the tax upon dividends of profit and loss corporations and have the tax base rest entirely upon the individual. This was also the position of U. S. Supreme Court Justice Louis D. Brandeis, who wrote the opinion for the four dissenting justices in the leading corporation tax case in the United States of Eisner v. McCumber.[21] For some incomprehensible reason, corporate business as a whole has failed to understand the principles involved and has carried on a war against the erroneously-termed "tax-exempt" cooperative. The income of a true marketing agent or agency is excluded from the income of the agency, corporate or otherwise, because it is in fact and law income of the principal.

The nonprofit corporation is used by many forms of individually owned businesses, ranging from individual grocers purchasing jointly to newspapers gathering news through the Associated Press. Individual consumers often use the same type of cooperative corporate entity for the purchase of insurance, hospitals, apartments, and an occasional grocery store. Farmers

[21]*252 U. S. 189 (1920)*

151

largely use this corporate entity to purchase vocational supplies and to market their products.

Double Taxation of Corporate Dividends Unjust: Should Be Abolished

It would appear that the time has come for Congress to reconsider the nation's method of levying business income taxes. All corporate, profit businesses except "small business corporations" electing to be taxed as members of a partnership are taxed under authorization of Subchapter S of the Internal Revenue Code are burdened as gratutious tax gathering devices for the government. Actually, what happens is that the stockholders who choose to operate the business for profit corporations must collect thirty per cent of net income up to and including $25,000.00 annually and fifty-two per cent of net income over $25,000.00 from the purchaser, who thus indirectly pays those amounts of income tax of the corporation as hidden taxes.

It is only after these payments that the profit corporation may then keep the remainder for its stockholders, who in turn pay a tax upon the portion distributed to them as dividends. *The corporation, of course, does not pay an income tax itself. It is merely the legally fictitious person which collects, and later remits taxes from those with whom it does business.*[22] In a recent article in *Fortune* Gilbert Burck states:

> Common sense and business habits tend to reinforce the supposition that the tax is shifted, partly or wholly, sooner or later, by some if not all companies. Regulated utilities are allowed to treat the tax as an expense in rate making, and usually do pass it on. Others try hard without benefit of regulation. Perhaps not one in five hundred executives could give, offhand, a thoroughly clear account of how he compensates for the tax. But for all

[22]*Murray D. Lincoln*, Vice President in Charge of Revolution *(New York, 1960), pp. 250-251.*

152

of them, getting around it is as routine as coming to work every morning. As Beardsly Ruml remarked to a *Fortune* editor just before he died, "Businessmen don't tell economists about how they pass the tax on and they don't tell Uncle Sam." And they probably don't even tell themselves; they just adapt to the tax, and the luckier and more skillful of them doubtless adapt better than the others.[23]

Any Steps To Force Cooperatives To Pay Taxes on Patronage Refunds Would Be Confiscation

The farm organizations have recognized the inequitable aspects of this situation and stand ready to help to rectify them. Profit and loss business, however, takes a position which can be summed up as follows: "We will continue to collect the tax gratis for the government, but we want incorporated partnerships or cooperatives to be compelled to do the same." But what private business claims that it wants is legally impossible. A true nonprofit corporation would be *ultra vires* if it made a profit from its member-patrons. A cooperative cannot legally make a profit when operating under a prior contract to act as the marketing, service, or purchasing agent of its members. If it makes a profit on nonmember business, it then becomes liable to the tax as though it were a profit corporation. If its patronage refunds were taxed, it would be a direct capital tax whether the refunds were in cash, merchandise, or in (*choses in action*) stock certificates. This is possible under the law of the Soviets. In reality, from a purely legal point of view, a tax upon refunds of overcharges would be a direct step toward Soviet state capitalism. Double taxation in this situation would constitute partial confiscation of the patron's property interest represented by a debt of the corporation to him without compensation to the patron.

[23]*Gilbert Burck, "You May Think the Corporate Tax is 'Bad,' But . . .,"* FORTUNE *(April 1963), 7.*

A Conservative Looks At Cooperatives

Tax Exemption Usually a Misnomer

It is interesting to note that the public generally, including many members of cooperatives, is confused upon the status of the nonprofit entity. When a corporation is organized as a nonprofit legal entity it does not need income tax exemption if it actually is incorporated in such a way that it does not produce profit income. Whether or not a statute gives income tax exemption to a true nonprofit corporation is really beside the point—such exemption is largely a matter of words—the statute confers no right that the corporation does not already possess because of its organization and type of operation under the principles of Anglo-Saxon law, as recently stated by the Supreme Court of the United States.[24]

The furor over income tax exemption largely results from a confusion in meanings exploited by those who do not want people to own and operate their own corporate agency.[25]

In 1889 in New York Life Insurance Co. v. Styles, *supra,*

[24]*The Internal Revenue Acts of October 20, 1951, and October 16, 1962, declared mandatory patronage refunds to be deductible by a cooperative. However, in James v. United States (366 U. S. 213, 1961), in which the majority of the United State Supreme Court held embezzled funds to be taxable to the embezzler, the Court made clear that an express agreement of debt requiring payment cannot constitutionally be taxable income to the debtor.*
[25]*Internal Revenue Code 1954, Sec. 216, allows as a deduction to individuals of amounts representing their proportion of taxes and interest paid to the cooperative housing corporation. This is typical of what is erroneously called tax exemption. The interested reader should also consult House of Representatives Report No. 1888 (April 9, 1946), titled "The Competition of Cooperatives with Other Forms of Business Enterprise." This report is one of the most thorough examinations of the charge that cooperatives enjoy tax exemption, and its conclusions completely support the role of the cooperative as a viable agent within a democratic society.*

Lord Watson stated the basic legal premise upon which so-called tax exemption for nonprofit mutuals or cooperatives rests. Lord Watson's decision is based upon the fundamental common law right of the free mobility of capital. To tax a refund would be tantamount to taxing a woman each time she moves her money from one handbag to another.

Lord Watson's decision states the case for all true cooperatives:

> The individual insured and those associated for the purpose of receiving their dividends [*refunds—Ed.*] and the pending policies when they fall in, are identical; and I do not think that their complete identity can be destroyed or even impaired by their incorporation. The corporation [*mutual—Ed.*] is merely a legal entity which represents the aggregate of its members; and the members of the Appellant Company are its participating policyholders.

W. L. Bradley, CPA, as Chairman of the Committee on Cooperatives, American Institute of Accountants, in 1946, wrote a brochure entitled "Taxation of Cooperatives" in which he condensed a lifetime of professional experience in dealing with the financial affairs of businesses, both profit and nonprofit. His evaluation of the place of the cooperative in the business world is as follows:

> . . . the cooperative movement is not aimed at the destruction of the system of free enterprise but, on the contrary, is a practical method of introducing needed correctives to a capitalistic, competitive economy of which it is a part. The cooperative offers a means by which individuals may gain, or regain, and assert ownership of enterprises and facilities through joint action with friends, neighbors, or like-minded persons, and by which they may have a voice in what they receive and what they pay.
> Definitely the cooperative movement does not seek to create monopoly but, on the contrary, seeks to destroy

only existing monopoly and, by its destruction, to restore health to the competitive system.[26]

Condominium

There are many ways in which persons may enjoy the results of their cooperative efforts without assuming the larger duties and responsibilities of participation in a *true* cooperative. One of these which has attracted much attention in recent years is known as a "condominium."

The condominium is a hybrid type of limited cooperative. For example an apartment house or other multiple unit building may be financed and constructed in such manner as to allow each person to own a dwelling or office unit in fee simple. This arrangement distinguishes it from incorporated cooperative building ventures, in which individuals secure assigned use rights by reason of ownership of stock in the corporation.

The quasi-cooperative is really not new. It has been in operation in some areas of Western Europe and Latin America for many years.

The primary individual ownership which condominium allows is its most attractive feature. Its disadvantages arise from the fact that there are several necessary services and utilities which must be operated and maintained in common. Because of the inability of a buyer to complete his purchase, or other difficulties, one unit may fall into disuse. Some participants may neglect to conform to the maintenance and operating requirements imposed upon all participants. The practical and legal difficulties of enforcement of neglected duties against a defaulting member of a nonstatutory condominium are very great.

At present, there is a definite trend in several states toward enactment of special legislation legalizing the formation of con-

[26]*Joseph G. Knapp,* Stokdyk—Architect of Cooperation *(American Institute of Cooperation, Washington, D.C., 1953), p. 211.*

156

dominiums. For example, in Utah, Pennsylvania, Florida, and Hawaii comprehensive acts have been adopted which enumerate in great detail the rights and duties of unit owners, the powers and duties of the management committee as agents of the unit owners, and numerous other details of this type of individual ownership with cooperation on maintenance and operation.[27]

It is not the purpose here either to indict or to endorse the condominium. It deserves careful study.[28] Perhaps over a period of time it may develop into a form of ownership and limited cooperation that, with proper safeguards, will come into general use. At the present time, however, the writer suggests a "Stop, Look, and Listen" attitude toward this type of hybrid quasi-profit cooperative.

[27]*Inasmuch as the concept of condominiums may be new to many readers, it is suggested that they refer to the following:*
State of Utah "Condominium Ownership Act," February 27, 1963; "Owning Without the Cares," BUSINESS WEEK (March 2, 1963) 81; United States Senate Banking and Currency Committee hearings, Testimony April 6, 1961, of D.D. Townsend; Housing Act of 1961—Report 281, May 19, 1961, 87th Congress, 1st Session.
[28]*An excellent and recent appraisal of the matter is the article by Arthur E. Warner and Alvin G. Becker entitled "Condominium," printed in BUSINESS TOPICS (Autumn, 1963), pp. 17-29.*

VII. Cooperative Operations and Procedures

"The acceptance of membership in a cooperative carries with it an obligation to study the workings of the organization, to become familiar with its business practices, to attend its meetings and to support actively its growth and welfare."

"A cooperative which fills a genuine economic need is built upon a sound foundation; one which does not is built upon the sand."

"While a cooperative is corporate in structure, it is also an entity for combining humanitarianism with business objectives."

1. Farmer Cooperative Policy and Management

Both private and public agencies have repeatedly pointed out that the farmer neither purchases nor markets efficiently. Too often, in the past, the farm family has toiled and labored, only to receive a "poverty return."

The single farmer by himself can do nothing to improve his business situation. America had to either repeat the mistakes of the past and permit the creation of a poor peasantry, or remedy the errors.

Farmer cooperatives had been tried in many places with varying degrees of success. Finally, in the early part of the century the federal government and the various state legislatures passed statutes authorizing farmers to form cooperative associations to fill the economic needs pointed out by the land grant colleges. In Canada similar legislation was passed by the Dominion and provincial legislatures.

159

A Conservative Looks At Cooperatives

The story of the farmer-owned cooperative in North America has never been completely told, much less understood. In these pages I should like to review some of the reasons for the successes and failures of the various cooperatives that have been formed since federal and state legislation authorized their existence.

Charter Outlines Functions

A farmer cooperative, like any other corporation, receives a charter from the state permitting it to organize and perform various business functions. Some of the best managed corporations in this country have a cooperative structure.

Capable Legal Talent Needed When Organizing

When a cooperative is in the process of being formed, a capable lawyer should be employed to assist in the organizational details. The lawyer selected should be well versed in the laws pertaining to cooperatives. It is unfortunate that there are not more such men in the country. There have been many instances where promising cooperative ventures have failed because of legal technicalities. Expensive litigation, resulting from faulty contracts or bylaws, has often frittered away the assets of the organization. Such situations have also resulted in unfavorable publicity. Proper legal advice at the outset may save a fledgling cooperative from much expense and embarrassment.

There should be a clear statement of the contractual relationship existing between the member or patron and the cooperative so that misunderstandings may be held to a minimum. It is imperative that either the articles of incorporation, the bylaws, or the contract between the member and his association carry a clause to the effect that it is mandatory that patronage savings or refunds be distributed; furthermore, the refunding of such monies should not be at the discretion of the trustees, directors, or management. This clause is of such importance that every cooperative should make certain that its wording has been approved by both the attorney and the auditor of the cooperative.

The articles of incorporation may be so drawn as to permit the cooperative to explore new and untried paths, if such exploration should prove desirable later. Corporate provisions should only be changed, however, after consultation with the membership and with outside advisory authorities. Strict conformity to the statutes and bylaws should be adhered to in every attempt to alter such provisions.

Often local civic pride—or entrenched cooperative officials—tends to discourage consolidation of cooperative facilities which, if consolidated, hold promise of more efficient operation and increased savings to member producers. The managers and directors who fail to recognize that cooperatives should cooperate with each other are violating their trust of office. They ought never to lose sight of the fact that the position of the official is *secondary to the interests of the organization as a whole and of the agricultural groups which the cooperatives have been created to serve.*

Base Cooperative Membership on Family Unit

Membership in a cooperative should be considered a family matter. Of course, one member of the family casts the vote and/or holds membership, but in most instances, the farmer discusses the problems of marketing his produce with his wife. Moreover, it is often the wife who balances the family budget. She has the chief responsibility for feeding and clothing the family and for guiding the education of the children. She must be convinced that membership in a cooperative is the correct solution for the family. If she is a "believer" she usually becomes the most loyal supporter of the cooperative.

Meetings for organizing cooperatives as well as subsequent membership gatherings should always include the man, his wife, and their adult children. Innumerable cooperative ventures have failed because the family was not "sold" on the project. The man alone did not have either the time or the ability to satisfy his family of the advantages of the cooperative.

The objective of the cooperative organization is to render service to patrons at cost. Both marketing and purchasing cooperatives render valuable service to their patrons and to the public, but their methods of cooperation are very different from each other. Every cooperator must make certain that his relation to the particular cooperative he is joining serves his need and that the organization functions democratically.

Reliable Audits Are Vital to Cooperative Success

There is a distinct need for proper bookkeeping techniques and adequate audits among the thousands of small cooperatives. Usual accounting and auditing procedures, applicable to profit-making commercial concerns, must be supplemented. Statutes dealing with cooperatives require cooperatives to follow certain special accounting and auditing procedures to protect the membership.

It is encouraging to note that the American Institute of Accountants, having become mindful of the problem, has appointed a standing committee to study the problem of cooperative accounting.[1] This committee, in collaboration with the American Institute of Cooperation, has already held accounting clinics in all sections of the country. In these clinics, leaders and policy-makers of farm cooperatives, state colleges and universities, banks for cooperatives, as well as public accountants, have examined together the specific accounting problems that face cooperatives.

[1] *The National Society of Accountants for Cooperatives has been organized to help develop accounting techniques and proper accounting terminology for cooperatives. Too often, terms of the profit world are used incorrectly in cooperative reports. Many times, reports are so complicated or of such a nature as to be misunderstood by farmer members who must make important decisions on the basis of these reports.*

Definite Procedures, Standards Needed for Directors

Cooperatives are headed by directors elected from among the members. A man or woman should assume the responsibility of directorship only if he is willing to undertake seriously the duties involved. Many cooperatives have had directors whose chief motives in accepting office were political, personal, or social. Such directors are only liabilities.

To be successful, cooperatives must follow a strict procedure in the election of directors. Some cooperatives elect directors to serve in managerial or executive positions. This should never be done without first polling the membership to gain their consent. Obviously there should never be any secrecy about it.

There are various methods by which the services and remunerations of directors are determined. The one inflexible rule is that nothing should be done without the full knowledge of the membership. A director should not assume office unless he is willing to have his ledger pages in the company's books open to examination by any member. The best way to prevent development of unfounded rumors is to let it be known that any member may examine the record of the director's business relations with the cooperative. Directors should attend meetings regularly.

Successful Businessmen Make Best Directors

New blood on the board of directors is good; on the other hand, many of the best cooperatives in the United States and Canada function without any system of rotating directors. The value of a director should increase with his experience, and, in the long run, members are the best judges as to who should be on the board. As a rule, competing business firms do not rotate directors—and remember, the cooperative is a business venture. However, due consideration should be given to adding new blood to the board.

Members of a director's or manager's family, either by birth or marriage, should be barred from employment in the cooperative. If any exception is made, it should be with the full knowledge and consent of the members at a regular meeting. Even though a director knows that his son is the best qualified person for the job, he should let someone else enjoy the services of the young man.

Executives, directors, and management of the association should not be financially interested in private facilities that furnish supplies or services to the group. There is an undercurrent of resentment among members whenever this type of operation exists, no matter how honestly administered.

Directors must supply the enthusiasm to keep the organization going. They must believe in cooperation. They must look upon it as an exemplification of, and a practical experiment in, Biblical ethics. They must "preach from the housetops." Through efficient operation, they must convince people that it is to their best interests to join cooperatives as members because of the mutual benefits involved.

Pick Reliable Manager; Make Him Fully Responsible

Directors must coldly evaluate the facts to determine what the cooperative needs in the way of management. They should hire the best possible manager and determine the salary to be paid in terms of what competitive business is paying for similar managerial services. A poorly paid manager is often a cooperative's most expensive luxury. A satisfied manager is usually a loyal manager. He should be well paid and then held strictly accountable for his performance. Needless to say, he should be a man of high capabilities, and not a businessman or farmer who has failed in his own ventures. The prospective manager's past business experience is important. A cooperative is hardly the place for a manager to change from a failure to a success.

Any cooperative large enough to have a paid manager requires a board of directors with enough good judgment to let the manager run the business within the policies established by the board. Many cooperatives have run into difficulties because the board has tried to take over managerial prerogatives. However, the directors should always actively determine policies and check with management to see that these directives are followed.

It has been true in some instances that, unless a board of directors has strong leadership, members are prone to get their hands into detailed operations which are the manager's job. More time will be spent discussing whether some employee should be given a $2.00 a week increase than considering important policy problems. The manager should hire and fire and run the business according to his best judgment.

Successful cooperative managers have a rare combination of theoretical and practical knowledge. On the other hand, many of the members know little about the actual operation of a commodity business. Members should be encouraged to discuss their individual problems with the manager. He, in turn, can help them become more interested in, and better informed about, the details of cooperative theory and operation.

Good Employee Relations Important

Wages should be in conformity with standard pay in the community. Cooperatives have no right to expect employees to serve for less than the pay obtainable from competitive business. Fortunately, there is a growing tendency among cooperatives to develop plans for annuities and to adopt other practices in conformity with good labor relations.

The whole labor problem, particularly as it affects the organization, should be continually studied. Heretofore, much difficulty has been experienced because of misunderstandings between labor and cooperators. Labor should be given an opportunity to learn the aims of the cooperative.

Successful Policymaking Requires Study by Committees

A number of the most successful cooperatives attribute their success and growth to careful policymaking by standing and special committees. Instead of having policies worked out by the manager or by an executive or advisory committee and immediately acted upon by the board, it is the practice of these cooperatives to refer suggested new policies to various committees for investigation and recommendation.

At a later date, committees present recommendations along with those of the manager to the board. This procedure assures careful consideration for each problem.

Management Must Meet Business World on Equal Terms

A good manager must be able to meet the business world on equal terms, neither giving nor asking favors. He must not insist on higher prices for his products "because farmers need them." Consumers are not interested in the sociological needs of agriculture as such. Nor must the manager of a purchasing cooperative expect concessions merely because his is a farmers group. He must purchase on the open market goods of at least the same quality as his competitors, and deliver them to the cooperative's patrons at a lower net cost. If he cannot do this, there is little justification for the cooperative's existence.

It is important that the manager realize the need to hold down his cost of doing business. In the last analysis, the member judges the cooperative by his net patronage returns or savings.

Savings, it must be remembered, include the intangible benefits of better quality. While savings of this sort cannot always be accurately determined in dollars and cents, they are one of the true benefits of cooperative action.

Consumers appreciate the values of properly graded products. The cooperative is uniquely able to pioneer and promote better grades. The cooperative exists to serve its membership and, as such, can make better grading a part of its regular operation. Ultimately this benefit is reflected in increased returns to farm families at no cost to others. Managers are becoming increasingly mindful of the great opportunity they have to render double service to members.

166

Manager Needs Wide Contacts

Real knowledge of the products handled in comparison with competing lines is essential. A manager should know the men interested in the same business, be they cooperative or other commercial representatives. He should carry on a wide correspondence and travel as extensively as possible, always keeping his eyes and ears open for ideas that may be translated into new services and savings for his members through increased efficiency in the management of the organization.

Travel of this nature and the necessary entertainment costs in connection with making and retaining important contacts are justified expense account items. In holding the manager responsible for results, directors must realize that, in forming new contacts with large buying and manufacturing groups, the manager makes many semi-social and semi-business contacts which involve considerable entertainment. This often results in expense accounts in excess of what the average director would regard as necessary.

Managers should refrain from adding frills to the business on their own initiative. The farmer-owners usually are more interested in immediate returns than they are in the possibilities of increasing their revenue by means of large facility investments. When it seems advisable that substantial expenditures be made, the matter should be discussed thoroughly with the board; and the board and management, in turn, should discuss the proposed expenditures with the members. Some cooperatives have found themselves financially handicapped by physical facilities that were much too large for their volume.

The successful manager lets his organization know what his plans are, thus forestalling their being misinformed through rumors.

Keep Members Informed

It is the joint responsibility of the board of directors and the manager to keep the membership informed regarding the business details of the organization. If the group is large enough, an association publication will be found most helpful. Such a house organ should contain suggestions of practical benefit to the members. A small organization can prepare a mimeographed report at a very small cost. The publication should be issued frequently. The more informed the membership, the more vigorous the organization.

Prompt Returns a Factor in Cooperative Success

Members have a right to expect, directors a duty to order, and managers an obligation to make payments as rapidly as sound business practice will allow. Just as honesty is the cornerstone of a successful cooperative institution, so prompt payment, both of initial returns from the crops delivered and of patronage refunds, is the keystone. Information and reasonable notice of the equities retained from savings or margins should be given to members at or near the time of retention.

Making overadvances is a practice which has been fatal to some cooperatives. In their eagerness to please their membership, many cooperatives have overadvanced and then have found at the end of the year that they have paid more than the returns justified. Assessments to rectify the mistake are hard to explain or collect.

Executives of the cooperative should furnish members a continual flow of information about what happens to their product after the seal is put on the freight car or truck door. Practically all primary agricultural products ultimately are sold in their raw or processed form over the counter of a chain, independent, or consumer cooperative store. These outlets are in direct and continuous contact with the consumers and their managers know who the consumer is for various products. Retailers, brokers, jobbers, and service wholesalers are usually willing to share such information. A reciprocating three-way flow of material information from the manager to directors and from manager and directors to members and vice versa is essential to a successful cooperative.

Keep in Touch with Retail Markets

Representatives of retail groups should be invited to visit cooperative meetings to explain consumer demands. Cooperative leaders should return these and get firsthand information on retail distribution.

Purchasing cooperatives should encourage conferences between their suppliers and cooperative executives to discuss potential farm needs and improvement of standards.

Keep Grades Based on Merit, Truth

Marketing cooperatives should build a reputation for grading their packs accurately. Only packs of highest quality should be so graded, and packs of inferior grades should not contain materials of less than the specified quality.

Cooperate with Other Agencies; Avoid Trade Fights

Discrimination against any particular form of wholesale or retail business, be it chain, independent, or consumer cooperative, by either legislative enactment or association boycott, is fundamentally wrong. Marketing cooperatives require all types of outlets as each fills the needs of a particular consumer group.

It is vital that cooperatives refrain from engaging in any controversy with or among industry groups. All types of buyers are potential customers for the marketing groups; purchasing cooperatives should regard all types of manufacturers as possible sources of supply.

When it is practical, cooperative officials should work with governmental agencies in setting up marketing agreements and other needed measures for the control of industry. Successful agricultural programs concern commodities largely handled by cooperatives.

Agricultural Colleges Proffer Much Aid

Agricultural colleges throughout North America are doing their best to help farmers. These institutions have available histories and case studies of the entire cooperative movement. Marketing experts on the staffs of the Extension Services are available to answer questions.

Too often, the farm groups, happy in their own ignorance, do not take advantage of this assistance. As a result, the cooperative dries up and finally dies.

Farm Credit Administration Should Be Consulted

Those interested in forming a cooperative should keep in close touch with the government agencies formed to assist in such matters. Too often, a cooperative has been formed without even consulting the Farm Credit Administration. Only when the cooperative finds itself in difficulty is this agency approached.

Cooperatives Must Stand on Own Feet

Cooperative directors and management should not cheapen their organization by undue solicitation for membership. A fair, informal, straightforward and courageous presentation of the facts, stressing the economic and social benefits, will do more to secure a lasting membership than painting too glowing a picture.

Cooperatives should not be used as a "front." Some early-day cooperatives were used merely to promote the narrow interests of particular cliques. A cooperative is doomed as soon as the membership realizes that it is being used for the private profit of an individual or corporation rather than for the good of its members. A cooperative can not serve two masters.

Good Public Relations Must Be Developed

The public relations of cooperatives are of paramount importance. Members, nonmembers, employees, governmental agencies, vocational schools, the clergy, and a score of other groups constitute the public of the organization. The cooperative cannot live alone. The best way to have the community understand the cooperative is to study the cooperative's place in the community itself. Much work needs to be done here; this is one of the great responsibilities of cooperative executives.

Area Farm Press Can Be Vital Ally

The press and radio in the area serviced by the cooperative should know that their representatives are welcome to visit the cooperative and attend its meetings. A friendly editor can do much to correct misunderstandings and create a friendly atmosphere for the cooperative. Too often he does not obtain his information from the cooperative itself. It is wise to make such editors allies.

Cooperatives and Their Future

Legislative enactments have favored the formation of cooperatives. Judicial decisions have given cooperatives wide powers. *With this grant of authority to the organization goes a responsibility, not only to its membership, but to the general public. Members, directors, and managers of cooperative organizations must recognize that other parts of the body politic are entitled to information about the organizations they guide. Public opinion, favorable to cooperative effort, can only be won when groups scrupulously operate within their grant of power and make a serious effort to serve the community and the nation as a whole.*

2. DIRECTORS AND THEIR CONSTITUENTS

All business corporations have a board of directors or trustees selected by stockholders or members and entrusted by the State with authority to conduct the affairs of the organization.[2]

[2]*Summary of remarks made by Raymond W. Miller at the Cooperative Association Clinic, The Pennsylvania State University, June 3-4, 1948.*

Most statutes define this as management or direction. The directors thus have a two-fold responsibility: one, to the State itself, which has granted the right to the corporate entity to do business; two, to the members or stockholders who have elected them.[3]

The responsibilities to the State are well defined, easy to ascertain, and should be followed to the letter. They include the making of reports, the payment of taxes, and the general supervision of the business. These functions normally are delegated to the manager, attorneys, accountants, etc., with the board of directors maintaining only supervision and enunciation of long-range policy.

The board should make certain that the financial activities of the corporation are examined and audited periodically by an accountant so that an honest financial statement will be readily available both for the State and for those who have a right to know its affairs. It must, in addition, keep itself informed of business conditions and of any changes in corporation law and statutes.

The member or stockholder constituency of the directors often is given too little thought. A person assuming duty as director of an organization should perform his duties on good faith and to the best of his ability. Often, however, the director does not understand that he has a continuing responsibility to the members or stockholders who elected him to office.

Duties of a director in this respect fall into various categories and classes. In general, he must keep himself fully informed about the proceedings of the business. However, he must not meddle in the affairs of management; his responsibility is to see that the policies of the board are being carried out and to be on the lookout for pitfalls. As far as possible, he should scout the road ahead.

[3]*The word "stockholder" will be used to denote either stockholder or member and the word "director" to mean either director or trustee of a corporation.*

The conscientious director will take every opportunity to get in touch with members or stockholders through meetings, private conversations, and letters. He will discuss at board meetings possible innovations in policy. He will learn the attitude of the members or stockholders of the organization to the policies presently in use and will, if he discovers that there is dissatisfaction, attempt to correct the situation by explanation and discussion.

Sometimes directors are under the impression that the business entrusted to them is small and of no great importance. No member or stockholder, they argue, has a vast stake in the enterprise. However, just as a savings bank is presumed to protect their customers, no matter how small their deposits, so the director of a cooperative should be no less responsible than bank officials. If it is of importance enough for him to accept the directorship, then it follows that the job should be well done. Many boards are cluttered up with men whose only interest is having their name on the letterhead. Even though the director receives no salary, his acceptance of the directorship means that he has obligated himself to doing the job.[4]

A board normally elects a president, a vice-president, a secretary, and a treasurer. Too often all affairs of the organization are left to this small group, the other board members becoming either rubber stamps or perennial objectors. Such a situation is not conducive to the best interests of the organization. It is important that the directors recognize that they cannot speak for the board as individuals, but can only act as empowered by the board as a whole. Away from directors' meetings, they are no different from any other member or stock-

[4]*Most boards of directors tend in practice to be self-perpetuating. Hence directors must assume the responsibility of self-discipline and self-examination. Periodically each director should catechize himself searchingly to determine if he is fulfilling his obligations and living up to commendable standards of conduct.*

holder of the organization. If a director makes decisions on his own initiative or attempts to commit the board without consulting it, he is acting in bad faith, which in this instance is synonymous with bad business.

A director is in a position to ascertain how the cooperative is regarded by the public at large. People will often discuss things frankly with him that they might not with employees. He should, therefore, be a good listener and assemble information which he can pass on to management meetings with the board in full session. An organization may perform with great efficiency and yet die because it neglects its public relations. Many corporations have saved themselves vast sums of money because their directors have been alert to changing public opinion. Continual thought must be given to the cooperative's relationships with the community.[5]

3. FAILURES OF FARMER COOPERATIVES

Farmer cooperatives have become an important part of the American economy. Yet while a growing and substantial

[5]*"The essential concern of corporation directors, particularly in our large corporations, is not today, nor should it ever have been, merely protection of stockholders and their interests. These functions are simply more in evidence than others. The problem is vastly more important. It is the reconciliation of private enterprise with the smooth functioning of a democratic society with justice to all groups: stockholders, executives, employees, creditors, customers, and the public. Such a broad concept of the functions of directors is frequently overlooked. Nevertheless, this should be the contribution of directors in our national life." John Calhoun Baker,* DIRECTORS AND THEIR FUNCTIONS *(Cambridge, Massachusetts, 1945), p. 138. On this entire subject of director responsibility Harvard University today stands out as the leader in promulgating effective philosophy and literature in that vital field. See Melvin T. Copeland and Andrew R. Towl,* THE BOARD OF DIRECTORS AND BUSINESS MANAGEMENT *(Cambridge, Massachusetts, 1947).*

minority of farmer cooperatives have successfully combined co-operation and sound business practices, a large majority of them have suffered from various business ills, and many have succumbed.[6]

Reasons Given for Discontinuance

Difficulties in the field of management	19.8%
Difficulties in the field of membership	19.7%
Natural or unavoidable causes (fire, crop failure, etc.)	10.9%
Insufficient business for efficient operation	10.3%
Financing and credit difficulties	9.6%
Transportation problems	9.1%
Opposition from competing enterprises	8.9%
Declining prices	5.4%
All others	6.3%

It is of more than passing interest that almost 60 percent of the failures were ascribed to "ineffective management." "High overhead" was the reason for 10 percent; "inadequate accounting and auditing," 4 percent; "dishonest officials," 3 percent; "one-man organization which failed when the man left," 2½ percent; "speculation," 2 percent; and a host of other reasons —including "looseness of organization," "lack of young members," "directors were managers' 'rubber stamp,'" "dissension among directors," "overpromotion by the organizers"—all of which were less than 2 percent of the total.[7]

It must be remembered that in many cases the reasons

[6]*Raymond W. Miller and A. Ladru Jensen, "Failures of Farmers' Cooperatives,"* HARVARD BUSINESS REVIEW *(Winter 1947).*

[7]*W. W. Cochrane and R. H. Elsworth,* FARMERS' COOPERATIVE DISCONTINUANCES, *Department of Agriculture, Farm Credit Administration, Miscellaneous Report No. 65 (Washington, D.C., 1943). A selected list of related articles is attached to the report.*

given may be superficial; real difficulties may have been much more complex. For purposes of clarity I shall treat the many deleterious factors involved in cooperative discontinuances under seven main headings: (A) failure to fill a vital economic need, (B) lack of the education that is necessary to create understanding and favorable attitudes of members, (C) financial difficulties, (D) defects in legal organization, (E) incompetent management and personnel, (F) improper operating methods and policies, and (G) miscellaneous deterrent factors.

A. *Failure to Fill Economic Need*

History teaches that cooperative associations have had their origin in the economic and psychological needs of their members. This has been particularly true in the development of the farm cooperative in America. But meeting the general needs which may justify the existence of the cooperative is not enough to insure the success of an individual organization. Futhermore, it is surely courting failure to organize a local cooperative mainly because of community pride or enthusiastic promotion. A cooperative should fill a specific economic need.

Too often the agricultural leaders who are chosen to consider the problems incident to forming a cooperative fail to make a careful investigation and study of the probable membership, the possible volume of business, the opportunity for market outlets, the risks inherent in fluctuating prices, the opportunity to obtain adequate capital, and the extent and probable intensity of the private-profit competition that will be encountered. Only when existing commercial facilities and services are inadequate or cost the producers too much for the services rendered, and when adequate membership, capital, volume of business, and market outlets can be secured, are the conditions favorable for the creation and continuance of a marketing or purchasing cooperative attuned to the needs of its prospective patrons. A cooperative is not assured of success merely because it can render a useful service. The moving spirits in the new business venture should make certain that the service proposed can be rendered effectively and economically, and that it is wanted by the local farmers.

It is, of course, true that not all the farmers in the area will join the cooperative no matter how much their membership is needed. Farmers are independent by vocation, and many of those who ought to be loyal cooperators will not become members of any association. Erich Kraemer and H. E. Erdman remark, "You can get one-third of the growers together in an organization; these can get another third to join; but no power outside the Almighty can draw the other one-third in."[8] Nevertheless the need must be widespread enough to enlist a membership adequate to support the organization.

Competition of Private-Profit Business. The organizers of a cooperative should take into account the private-profit enterprises with which the association must compete. Unless the cooperative can demonstrate a greater ultimate return or saving to the patron, it will have a precarious existence.

At the same time, the effect of types of competition must be discounted. Aside from the boom periods of war prosperity, farmers generally are a low-income group. They ordinarily need and are tempted by the prospect of ready funds. A little higher cash price from the commission merchant than the long-time, estimated returns from the cooperative is an attractive lure to a needy farmer. Profit interests frequently oppose a new cooperative movement in various ways. The organizers should contemplate the continuing need of farmers for cash and anticipate that dealers will offer an advance of money on crops and bind the producers by contracts to sell exclusively to them. Commis-

[8]*Erich Kraemer and H. E. Erdman,* History of Cooperation in the Marketing of California Fresh Deciduous Fruits, *University of California, College of Agriculture, Bulletin No. 557 (September 1933), p. 120, quoting from a speech by a "Mr. Gordon" at the Thirtieth Fruit Growers' Convention, December, 1904.*

sion merchants usually handle several lines of products and can temporarily forego profits, or even lose money on one commodity, in their endeavor to put a cooperative out of business. A study made by the University of Minnesota in 1926 of the difficulties of a newly formed poultry producers' cooperative revealed:

> The former middlemen were active in inciting suspicion among cooperative members. They did this at times by publishing propaganda, but mainly by circulating rumors and occasionally by quoting irregular prices on eggs.[9]

B. *Lack of Education of Members*

Most farmers work hard and long against the stubborn, hazardous forces of nature to earn a livelihood for their families. The physical weariness that follows each day of hard work leaves little opportunity for self-motivated education. This is one of the reasons why cooperative education takes hold slowly.

Various studies disclose that farmers generally do not understand the nature and the long-term purposes and benefits of cooperatives.

Propaganda versus Education. The few who understand cooperative marketing and purchasing, but do not understand the deeper implications in the proper dissemination of cooperative philosophy, find it easy to use the political method of propagandizing the farmer with generalizations and promises. Those who realize the true significance of cooperatives educate patiently and insist on giving the real facts. Mr. John Pickett, who was at one time editor of *Country Gentleman* and is now editor of the *Pacific Rural Free Press,* wrote me as follows:

[9]*Carl C. Zimmerman and John D. Black,* The Marketing Attitudes of Minnesota Farmers, *University of Minnesota, Agricultural Experiment Station, Technical Bulletin No. 45 (December 1926), p. 34.*

In my experience, one of the great weaknesses of cooperatives is their lack of good public relations—their propaganda about themselves, boasting and boosting themselves, instead of doing their members the compliment of giving them the facts, and letting them base their judgment upon the facts frankly given and accepted as sincerely by the members.

Education, when the educator cannot be in regular contact with the persons to be educated, when he cannot make assignments of study material, and when he cannot compel study by checking the student's mastery of the subject, is hardly education at all. We have not yet built a program of effective adult education as the Scandinavian countries have done. The remarkable work of the land grant colleges, of the various farm organizations, of the Future Farmers Associations, and of the 4-H Clubs is helping to educate rural America to the need for better business organization among farmers. Yet progress here seems to move at a snail's pace. For the time being we can expect some cooperatives to over-emphasize the anticipated benefits of cooperation; managers often feel they must be optimistic to retain their popularity.

Members' Attitude Toward Management. A partially informed, emotionally propagandized group is usually a suspicious group. Moreover, a group lacking full confidence in those to whom they entrust their business interests will be at best partially unified and mildly loyal. Then too, human attitudes are ever in a state of flux between personal interest and group welfare. Jealousy is a frequent and evil companion of suspicion; both jealousy and suspicion thrive on ignorance. A marked hindrance, therefore, to the strength of agricultural cooperatives is found in the members' attitude toward their management.

In the survey made by the University of Minnesota in 1926 regarding the marketing attitudes of Minnesota farmers, 17.7 percent of the farmers interviewed stated that they would not join a cooperative because they thought the management might

179

not be trustworthy.[10] This suspicion was not well founded. The exhaustive survey of the Farm Credit Administration showed that apparently less than two-thirds of one percent (0.64 percent, to be exact) of total cooperative failures were due to dishonest officials. Nevertheless we must reluctantly conclude that even where good public relations are coupled with good management, the suspicion of management by nonmember farmers in the area is a significant factor contributing to cooperative discontinuances.

Furthermore, members are likely to show a niggardly attitude in the matter of compensation. Farmers with small incomes are often not psychologically conditioned to favor salaries which are merited by, and needed to secure, capable managing officers who can compete effectively with private profit enterprise. They are likely to feel somewhat the same way about the organizers of a cooperative.

The task of organizing a marketing or purchasing cooperative is a difficult one. It requires ability, belief in the cooperative movement, and a great expenditure of time, energy, and money. Few farmers are in a position to meet all these requirements. Innumerable farm cooperatives have failed to secure and retain adequate membership, partly because members and prospective members objected to the fact that some of the farmer-promoters were to receive a small compensation for their activity.

In the commercial world, legitimate promoters of business ventures are allowed a salary, a commission, or a share in the business as stockholders. Such rewards are approved as a matter of common practice. The farmer often thinks differently. Only reluctantly does he approve adequate salaries for managing officers or usual fees for professional services of attorneys and accountants. The farmers' psychology in this regard is difficult for persons in other businesses to understand. It is not in any way a personal fault of the farmers, but primarily a reflection

[10]*Zimmerman and Black, p. 34.*

of their quasi-isolated environment, their hard life, and low incomes. Nevertheless it remains one of the intangible reasons why some cooperatives have not succeeded. Here again is a problem of educating farmers to business ideas and practices, which in the long run will benefit their own economic position.

Personal Independence. The attitude of personal independence is so strong in many farmers that it is difficult to persuade them to join with others in marketing their products. The idea of gaining a small personal advantage, rather than accepting common returns with the larger group, expresses itself in several ways:

(a) Some growers have the ability, by staying out of a cooperative, to make special deals with private concerns and thus receive higher prices for their commodities than the members of the local cooperative receive for theirs. Such operators, realizing that a cooperative stabilizes the market, take advantage of the competitive bidding of private-profit business and thus jeopardize the existence of the very cooperative which provides them such temporary advantage.

(b) The earlier cooperatives had marketing contracts for a period of years without any annual option of withdrawal. These earlier contracts were a source of discontent to many members who did sign such contracts. The cooperatives have largely solved the problem by granting a brief period each year within which notices of withdrawal are valid, or by allowing some private profit dealing upon payment of modest liquidated damages to the cooperative.

(c) The recent development of fast-moving trucks and modern highways, airplanes, and less-than-carload-lot shipments gives growers an opportunity to cover vast distances quickly, thus permitting speculation in many markets. Often, higher immediate prices are secured in this way than would be possible through the local cooperative. The desire of some farmers to seek these advantages is a deterrent to the strength of the

181

local cooperative. Such activity, however, sometimes causes a distant market to be demoralized, which tends to lessen the injury to cooperatives by these speculative practices.

C. *Financial Difficulties*

Organization of a new corporation is costly; training of new business personnel is likewise expensive. No business can have a stable existence until it is supplied with adequate permanent capital facilities, an adequate operating fund, and reasonable reserves for necessary purposes. This is true also of cooperative associations, most of which start as small, independent, local enterprises. In too many cases it has proved difficult to secure requisite capital and reserves from members who were already hard pressed for personal funds. This difficulty gave rise to the revolving-fund method of capitalizing cooperative corporations. The accumulation of a fund through the retention by the cooperative of a small percentage of the net return on each unit of produce sold has proved to be an important method for building the corporate capital which has enabled many cooperatives to survive. When enough capital for financial safety has been secured, the cooperative may begin to revolve the fund by paying the first returns to those producers from whom the margins were received.

With cooperatives that are not adequately capitalized at the time of organization, it is important for the management and membership to learn the advantage of building an adequate capital by retention of an ample percentage of net margins, which may be evidenced by certificates of interim capital units or by certificates of indebtedness to patrons. These may be redeemed or paid to patrons on a revolving plan when the financial security of the cooperative permits such cash disbursement.

A most significant step toward financial stability for cooperative enterprises was taken when Congress provided for the creation of the Central Bank for Cooperatives and the twelve regional Banks for Cooperatives in the Farm Credit Administration Act of June 16, 1933. Not only did this Act enable sound cooperatives to gain valuable financial aid, but the banks created by it have served as indirect advisory and educational agencies to cooperatives on financial policy and as a yardstick to private banks in making loans to cooperatives. These banks are a strong factor in minimizing cooperative discontinuances in the United States and in stabilizing our agricultural economy. The costs and expenses of operating the Banks for Cooperatives are paid out of the interest received by the Banks for Cooperatives from loans made by them to cooperative associations.

Undue Expansion. Another important reason for the failure of a cooperative is often an ill-advised or poorly planned attempt to enter the processing of raw farm products into consumer finished goods. Cooperatives which go extensively into processing or manufacturing may encounter several serious obstacles. Inadequate financing, lack of experience, and lack of competent personnel are among the troubles that beset them. Manufacturing operations require a specialized type of experience and personnel. Management may have difficulty in recognizing and securing the right kind of skilled workers to conduct the processing or manufacturing operations.

There is, too, the matter of competition from established concerns which are jealous of any encroachment in their field. Those companies are experienced competitors and do everything possible to close trade channels to the articles manufactured by the new competitor. Farmers needing returns from crops in order to finance ordinary operations are often not in a position to withstand a prolonged trade war involving a manufactured commodity. Furthermore, if the competitive operations are efficient (which is much more likely to be the case with private-profit manufacturing enterprises than with private businesses in the agricultural marketing field), then there is not a genuine economic need for the cooperative to fill.

Cooperative manufacturing enterprises with an unusual

combination of understanding membership, good management, and adequate financing have succeeded. The present trend is toward an increase in such integrated businesses under sound management and enlightened membership.

D. *Defective Legal Organization*

About a fourth of the earlier cooperatives were voluntary unincorporated associations. These loose-knit organizations were not separate business entities, but large unwieldy partnerships imposing full personal liability upon each member and being legally dissolved by the death of a member. This type of association has proved to be an unstable business unit even for private-profit businesses. Numerous cooperatives failed because they lacked the strong legal ties, the stability, and the efficient operation furnished by a nonprofit corporate form of organization with its separate legal personality, perpetual succession of membership, and freedom from personal liability of its members. The study of the Farm Credit Administration reveals that 23.4 percent, or almost one out of every four, cooperative discontinuances in the United States involved unincorporated associations.[11]

E. *Defects in Management Policies*

Although the cooperative may be given a perfect legal blueprint by which to operate, it is vital to have competency in management and in personnel and public relations. The difficulty in securing the right management and then making sure that it is supported by able directors is a prime cause of cooperative failures.

Expert managers are scarce. It is sometimes difficult for farmers to select a manager who will work with the trade and who will at the same time protect the producers' interests. Fre-

[11]*W. W. Cochrane and R. H. Elsworth, Farmers' Cooperative Discontinuances U.S.D.A. Misc. Rep. No. 65 June 1943.*

quently after a cooperative has been formed the members are so anxious to hire a manager at an insufficient salary that untried men or those who have failed in other ventures are placed in charge. Similarly, promotions, even for capable managers, are too often unduly delayed or forgotten entirely.

F. *Financial Management*

When a farmer entrusts his products or money to a cooperative organization, its management and directors assume a moral and legal responsibility to handle his business as scrupulously as a trust company does that of its beneficiaries. In a great many instances, cooperatives have failed because a proper accounting system was considered too expensive. Most organizations with larger memberships manage this problem adequately, but some of the most needless failures in the cooperative field have resulted from improper bookkeeping and inadequate year-end audits in cooperatives having a small membership.

Good business practice requires that the directors arrange for an outside firm of auditors, preferably with some experience in cooperative matters, to make an annual independent audit of the cooperative's books. Only in this way can the directors and members be assured that proper accounting methods are being used and that financial acts of the manager are substantiated by acceptable records.

G. *Miscellaneous Difficulties*

The number of tenant farmers in the United States militates against larger memberships of farmer cooperatives. Tenants often need immediate cash for their crops. Furthermore, they hesitate to invest any of their money in cooperative facilities because of the possibility that they may soon have to leave their farms. Sometimes, too, lessors reserve in the lease the right to market the entire crop, allowing the tenant to share with them in the proceeds. Cooperatives grow where freeholders live. They do not easily take root among tenant farmers. But today there are encouraging signs in the opposite direction. After all, tenants need cooperatives as an aid in becoming freeholders— which in itself is in the interest of national welfare.

Need for "Two-Way Service." It should be recognized that a farm is really a manufacturing plant where fertilizer, seed, air, sunshine, and hard work are mixed, with the aid of the chemical processes of photosynthesis, to create agricultural products. However efficient the production may be, there can be no success without efficient purchasing and marketing. Cooperatives can, however, operate a two-way service, thereby increasing the size and strength of the cooperative.

Conclusion

A farm cooperative is basically the marketing and purchasing agent of the farmers and not just another corporation. Failure to appreciate this truth has been the greatest single factor inhibiting the success of cooperatives. A farm cooperative is corporate in structure, but its business objectives are combined with humanitarianism. It is a creature of the state organized in the interest of the general welfare for the purpose of aiding agriculture and developing a balanced national economy. Its members should be producers not only in fact but in spirit. Its directors should be men who recognize that agricultural cooperation and national welfare are synonymous. Its managers should be good business executives, who, in addition, have a deep interest in human welfare in general and in agricultural stability in particular.

While the cooperative must, of necessity, do business in the public market place, the commodity exchange, and at the wholesale terminals, its policy makers must never forget that the cooperative is definitely rural in its program and heritage. When these factors are not taken into consideration, the cooperative becomes more or less a "country club" organization; the directors no longer concern themselves with the problems of the average producer, and management loses interest in human values. When this happens, the cooperative finds it has sown the seeds of its own undoing.

The last paragraphs of the Farm Credit Administration report previously mentioned pertinently sum up the whole program of the successes and failures of farm cooperatives. They read:

> Many cooperatives are more than organizations for selling and buying commodities and obtaining services. They are community institutions which handle commodities, take in and pay out money, distribute savings, carry on educational work, promote wholesale recreation, maintain morale, and promise much in the way of a better economic system.
>
> When one of these institutions closes its doors, the repercussions are more far-reaching than when a private profit concern handling about the same volume of business ceases to operate. The discontinuance of a cooperative directly affects a relatively large number of individuals—the member-patrons who are the owners of the enterprise. The loss of the invested capital falls upon them as does also the loss of the intangible benefits derived from working together. In addition to the loss of accumulated savings, the shock to the community frequently inhibits it for some time from further efforts in behalf of improved economic conditions. This impairment of morale, although not easily measured, is a loss that is both social and economic.
>
> Cooperation as an economic technique does not fail as frequently as do the men and women who attempt to use this technique without knowledge of its limitations as well as its many possibilities. Their sins of commission and omission are many. The greatest of these is that they have not mastered the fundamental principles of cooperation nor schooled themselves sufficiently in the application of those principles. Another of their shortcomings is that they have not practiced the art of cooperating

187

sufficiently to acquire a reasonable stock of cooperative experience.

Records discredit any idea that cooperation is a failure, even though some individuals may fall short. Farmer cooperation is a success and the immediate task is primarily that of orienting all would-be cooperators, whether they wish to market their crops or purchase their supplies through cooperative enterprises.

4. RESEARCH—THE MOST VITAL TOOL IN THE ADMINISTRATOR'S WHOLE WORKING KIT[12]

One dictionary defines research as "diligent and systematic inquiry or investigation into a subject to discover facts or principles." Another dictionary defines research as "the exploration of the unknown to gain factual information and to devise better ways to do things."

However you define it, research is as old as mankind. Someone in the dim dead past explored the unknown, made diligent inquiry into the subject, and finally figured out how he could keep himself snug and warm by heat outside of his body, in addition to the internal bodily reactions to food and exercise.

Through research, someone a long time ago learned that it was much easier to move a heavy load by placing it on a slab of wood than to try to pick up the load and carry it.

Through research, someone discovered that wheels are vastly superior for moving a heavy load than a skid.

In due time, man discovered the power which comes when water reaches the boiling point and changes into steam. Through research, he learned how to apply the power of steam to transporting heavy loads and to doing the world's work.

In the past hundred years, research has resulted in tremendous advances in the prevention and cure of diseases, and in gains in sanitation and nutrition. The average span of life

[12]*Published originally in the* MANAGEMENT QUARTERLY *of the National Rural Electric Cooperative Association, Washington, D.C. (March 1962).*

has jumped from forty to seventy years.

Prior to the middle of the nineteenth century, most research was carried on for the purpose of war. The hermetically sealed jar for preserving food, for instance, was evolved and perfected to win a prize offered by Napoleon, who wanted some way to provide fruit for his troops during his Russian campaign. The first system of mass production in America was developed to turn out Springfield rifles in quantity for the Civil War.

Research for business and industrial purposes—and for the good of society—has really come into its own since World War II. Research today is the most vital and, at the same time, the most necessary tool in the businessman's whole working kit.

In his popular lecture, "The Greatest Thing in the World," Henry Drummond quoted the scientist who discovered chloroform as saying that any book in his field of science more than ten years old was not worth keeping and should be discarded. Books on science technology and particularly on atomic energy go out of date much faster than that these days.

The business manager or the administrator who does not recognize he is living in changing times, who does not see the need for research, who does not encourage and promote research in his own and related fields, is on the way out.

Research need not be excessively expensive if it is carefully planned. The amount of money to be spent for research should be budgeted at a fixed and reasonable proportion of an organization's revenue. The organization itself must determine what that proportion should be, and for what specific purposes the money is to be spent.

Some organizations do their own research. Others conduct their research with their trade association group. Still others utilize the services of outside consultants and university research facilities.

There is, however, one important thing to remember. Research up till now has been very largely in the field of the mechanical, physical and biological sciences. Too little time and thought have been devoted to genuine research in the field of the humanities.

Consider a cooperative organization whose membership is rapidly changing in numbers and in vocation, changing, for instance, from rural to urban. Can such an organization expect to keep its head above water, if it does not make effective use of research to find how to adjust to changing conditions and to find new ways to serve its members?

Can an organization whose members are also its customers continue to have the loyalty and support of those members, if it does not recognize that its membership is never static but virtually a parade?

Can a cooperative organization afford not to engage in research in the field of membership relations to determine exactly what its members want done and how to do it?

Can a cooperative organization afford not to engage in research to find better ways to be more friendly and understanding and to gain greater acceptance on the part of the various segments of the public?

Can a cooperative organization in this day and age afford to ignore national affairs and world affairs and feel that the solution of national problems and world problems can best be accomplished by the government?

There can, of course, be no fixed program of research for all organizations. Each organization must work out its own program. And each organization must decide how much it is willing to appropriate for research. My suggestion would be that an organization devote 5 percent of its revenue to research. Three-quarters of this amount should be spent for pure material and procedural research and one-quarter for research in the field of human relations.

But whatever the amount decided upon, it is important to keep in mind that research today is the organization manager's most vital working tool.

190

EPILOGUE

1. The Man with the Hoe

As a boy, I lived in San Jose, California. Just a few blocks from us lived a white-haired poet, who had just written a poem that had already made him famous. The poem was "The Man With The Hoe," and the author's name was Edwin Markham.

Markham was a great friend of my grandmother, Mrs. E. H. Pound, who enjoyed and encouraged discussion, and he spent many evenings in our family circle. We used to persuade him to recite some of his verses and once after he had gone home, my grandmother said to me, "Raymond, some day you will be part of the new world that Edwin Markham is helping to create. Words move men's souls to action, and Markham's words spell eternal truth."

And so it has been. His immortal poems have served to inspire millions then unborn to look above the clods under their feet and think, and dream, and plan, and create. People the world over have come to realize that the world can be improved and made a better one for their children.

Perhaps the best known lines from Markham's "The Man With The Hoe" are these:

> Bowed with the weight of centuries he leans
> Upon his hoe and gazes on the ground,
> The emptiness of ages in his face,
> And on his back the burden of the world.

2. The Man With Hope

In this book I have attempted to portray the nonprofit corporation as a living legal tool that can be used by many for the common good. Cooperatives are created to be trail blazers for a better world.

In this day of rapidly developing social, economic, and political change, cooperatives offer the only possible seedbed in which private capitalistic business can take root and grow.

191

The newer lands do not have the capital to create profit-and-loss businesses, as we know them. Their only avenues for development are through a government becoming totalitarian, or through the citizens themselves developing self-help organizations to provide necessary capital and capital assets.

The cooperative, as a seminar for democracy, can help people gain capital and experience. If the state alone is responsible for the nation's development, it cannot be forced out save by armed revolution.

Because cooperatives are of the people themselves, they generate hope and confidence and self-reliance, the very stuff of which democracy is made. Cooperation is the science and art of many working together for common comfort, culture, and convenience.

Today's cooperator, the modern-day contemporary of Markham's man with a hoe, by turning his face upward, can envision a new and better world created through the joint effort of himself and his peers, as they work together.

Working through cooperators, he will help preserve our hard-won freedom for generations to come.

Perhaps, by the year 2000, Edwin Markham's successor will write even more stirring verses and entitle them "The Man With Hope Fulfilled."

ACKNOWLEDGEMENTS

I am fortunate in having two types of libraries—one, of friends scattered in the four corners of the earth; the other, of books on my own shelves and in the stacks of the Harvard Graduate School of Business Administration. In the preparation of this manuscript I have leaned heavily upon both types of libraries. Those books and other publications that have been quoted are acknowledged in footnotes and other references. I owe a debt to the authors of these works, some of whom I know, and others who are mere names to me. However, to a few in my "library of friends" I owe a debt of thanks that I can never repay. Two of these persons, Wallace J. Campbell, Vice-President of CARE and the Director of Public Affairs for Nationwide Insurance Companies, and Dr. Joseph G. Knapp, Administrator of the Farmer Cooperative Service of the United States Department of Agriculture, were the immediate cause of my writing this book.

From former President Herbert Hoover, I received not only publication permissions, but more importantly, his encouragement to go through with the project. From Raymond J. Mischler, Assistant to the Assistant General Counsel for the Department of Agriculture, and Lyman S. Hulbert, attorney at law and authority on cooperative law, came many of the suggestions for the chapter "Cooperatives and the Law."

Two friends, even though now deceased, have left their mark on this book: Charles Teague, former president of Sunkist, whose inspiration many years ago showed me the importance of cooperatives as a vital force in democracy; and Herbert R. Grossman, my law associate for many years, whose helpfulness is reflected in many pages of this book.

My son and associate, Robert W. Miller, not only helped in researching much of the material on Puerto Rico and Canada, but also assumed many duties of our joint business operations so that I might be free to complete the writing of these pages.

The results of a public relations audit which he directed for a group of mid-continent cooperatives in 1956 has also been extensively drawn upon in arriving at many of the conclusions contained in this book.

Ray Zimmerman, our associate and the former president of the Society for the Advancement of Management, whose pioneering efforts in providing group health insurance on a cooperative basis have gained him respect in the medical community as well as among consumers, gave unstintedly of his time in helping me develop these materials.

I have also received many of the ideas on these pages from my brother, David W. Miller, whose observations were based on experience as a successful farmer in California, and as a member, director, or executive officer of several nonprofit organizations.

Dr. A. Ladru Jensen, Professor of Corporation Law at the University of Utah, and my long-time colleague in legal explorations into the basis of cooperative law, is due my thanks for his forthright criticism of much of the material in this work. As a master legal craftsman, his suggestions were perceptive and valid.

Dr. Taylor Culbert, Director of the Ohio University Press, is due my gratitude for his labors in producing a finished book from the various manuscripts that I submitted to him.

Miss Florence Glynn, Financial Aid Officer of the Harvard Graduate School of Business Administration, and member of the Board of Directors of the Harvard University Credit Union, has my sincere thanks for her meticulous typing of the several drafts.

Finally, William L. Robinson, Associate Director of Traffic Engineering and Safety for the American Automobile Association, Book Architect, and my associate for many years, has my thanks and appreciation for his inspired assistance. His fine editorial touch is shown in every paragraph. Without his efforts, all the work of the rest of us would have been in vain.

194

ABOUT THE AUTHOR[1]

Shri Achmuru laid the ancient iron hoe carefully against a bind (levee) and stood with eyes narrowed to watch the three men coming up the path toward his onion patch. One of the three strangers was a Westerner. The little Hindu farmer raised his hands before his face, fingertips touching in the signal of friendship, and bowed.

The Westerner returned the greeting with the others. His hands, Shri Achmuru observed, were square and strong. The fingers were work-seamed. The spaces about his eyes, the muscle lines of his neck bore the pleasing brown mask the sun bestows upon men of the land.

This hatless sahib, one of the trio was explaining, was a visitor from America. Shri Achmuru held his tongue in politeness.

Had not this American stooped casually to pluck a grass-stalk from the path's edge? Was he not chewing it, hands in hip pockets, while his grave eyes stared up and down the onion rows and across to the iron hoe, and back again? There was no need for words here. The identification was complete.

Quickly, Shri Achmuru reached to the ground, scooped up a handful of his loam and handed it to the American. "Ask this sahib," he said, "where he has farmed. Never before have we seen an American farmer. We have been told that all Americans are rich capitalists, riding in great iron machines and despoiling the land. But he is like one of us."

Dr. Raymond W. Miller of Linden, California, one of the globe-wandering Rural Consultants of the Food and Agricultural Organization of the United Nations, rubbed the handful of soil carefully between his fingertips.

[1]*From Robert West Howard, "The Ramparts We Sow,"* THINK *(January 1951), 3 ff. Reprinted by permission of* THINK, *copyright 1950, by International Business Machine Corporation.*

"Tell Mr. Achmuru," he said, "that farmers are pretty much alike everywhere on earth. We all work with the dirt, the sun, and the rain. It's a brotherhood with emblems and symbols that can't be concealed. I began hoeing gardens when I was six years old and drove a waterwheel when I was eight, with a mule rather than a camel. In America, we farmers are capitalists in the sense that we own our land. But we are landsmen, too."

Shri Achmuru said slowly in reply, "It is a wonder I have often had. But, alas, when one cannot read, there is only rumor and gossip, too often by men of selfish interest. I am asking too much, perhaps, for the sahib's time must be of great value. Could he, perhaps, examine my onions from the American standpoint and—if only for a moment—tell us what is this mule and the other farm machines of which we have heard so much?"

Sensing the meaning of Shri Achmuru's gestures, Dr. Miller reached for a little hoe and with one chop deftly lifted an onion and its root structure up from the soil. "Poor stock to begin with," he said peering at the spindly roots. "More than that, he seems to have mineral deficiencies in his soil. Bullock manure, a legume crop and better seed should fix him up."

Shri Achmuru's eyes clouded as the analysis was repeated to him. "These I had intended for a cash crop. With them I hoped to buy the things my soil needs. Perhaps you can advise me." He paused, stared sidelong toward the American again. "Will he tell us about the mule and of farming in America? If he could speak but for a short while, I shall have the chair brought."

The translator, a young official of the Indian Department of Agriculture, repeated the question in English. Ray Miller nodded again and started to speak. But the words were drowned by a shrill halloo from Shri Achmuru, accompanied by a waving of arms. There were returning shouts from neighboring fields.

The translator, lips compressed to hold back laughter, said, "You are about to lecture the entire village. That is, as soon

196

as the chair arrives. It is the custom, when a Westerner visits an Indian village, he always occupies a chair. No dignitary from the West would sit on the ground as our farmers do."

Dr. Miller eased himself to the grass at the edge of the onion patch. "Dirt," he grunted, half to himself, "has supported man for two million years. It's still good enough."

Shri Achmuru's eyes popped at the sight. Then, the smile furrowing his face, the little Hindu walked to Dr. Miller's side, bowed, uttered a laughing sentence and sat down. The translator smiled and seated himself next to them. "The phrase he just used is a colloquialism," he said. "Loosely translated, it is as you say, 'Well, now I have seen everything.'"

The rest of the villagers came to the edge of the patch, stared unbelievingly, then seated themselves.

Dr. Miller began, "I am glad you asked about the mule, for it has one thing in common with the farmer. Both the farmer and the mule are of high intelligence. Neither works blindly. Both must be reasoned with. In Asia there are few mules. But farmers are everywhere in the world. Despite the great cities, the farmer still forms two-thirds of the world's population. And, because he is of high intelligence, he must proceed from understanding and from ideas. He is proud. He seeks the full freedom and happiness that land and ownership of land can give him. There, he knows, lie neighborliness and friendship. This, I ask you, always remember, for it is a highway to world peace.

"Now as to this mule: the Americans borrowed it from Spain, just as we borrowed the cucumber, the eggplant, the onion and sugarcane from your ancestors here in India . . ."

It was almost sunset when the meeting broke up. To a rapt audience, Dr. Miller had described tractors, wire fencing, mineral fertilizers, marketing agreements and even the flavor of maple syrup. He explained the global idea-swapping program started in 1947 by FAO's fieldmen and the resulting introduction of windmills and truck gardens in Egypt, hybrid corn in

197

India, brown rice in the Philippines and East Indies, better fish ponds in America and reforestation projects in Palestine and Arabia.

So, in the lengthening shadows, Shri Achmuru made the speech of farewell in the name of all the village.

"Whispers from the north have grown to open talk," he said. "There are many hereabouts who say that the hammer-and-sickle would bring us equality and more land. But this sickle of their symbol has long been a sign of slavery to us. India's farmers, too, are like your wonderful mules. We want the reasons and the ideas. Give us those and we will find something greater than equality. We will find freedom. Gifts like yours enable us to look other men in the eyes as brothers, not as fawning beggars or thieves who take from others and give nothing in return. If your way is that capitalist democracy of which they speak, then it is for us also."

Ray Miller and the interpreter sat in silence in the rear seat of the car as it lurched down the dirt road toward Delhi. The American stared at his hands, lying limply in his lap. France, Italy, Syria, Egypt, Pakistan, Siam, the Philippines—everywhere he had heard similar words, as blunt and direct as the soil and wind themselves. Minds couldn't help but ponder . . . in the silences . . . when world peace was in issue. Two-thirds of the world's population are still farmers. In their hands, in the final analysis, rests the power to swing humanity into paths toward cooperation and freedom.

DEFINITIONS

Nonprofit corporations are legal entities created to serve their member patrons at cost. They serve in a multitude of purposes, and have been subject to varying nomenclature. Some writers have called them incorporated partnerships, some a corporation not for profit, others just call them cooperatives with the distinctive meaning which that term is fast coming to possess. Correct nomenclature in law and business is indispensable. It is the means by which clarity of thought and communication is achieved. Good semantics are necessary for a more accurate understanding of the different functions and patron services of profit and nonprofit corporations.

There are a few words and phrases used in the business world which are common to both the profit and the nonprofit corporation, while some terms are distinctly a part of the vocabulary of one or the other of these types of corporations. No attempt is made in the book to define all of these words. However, there are a few words whose exact meaning, as intended by the author, should be known to the reader:

CAPITALISM

Capitalism is that form of business enterprise developed in the twentieth century that participates in producing economic progress through social justice by democratic means, or, as Brooks Hays defines it, "Capitalism is private enterprise with a conscience."

CARTELS AND TRUSTS

These are combinations of firms or other organizations whose objective is to limit the supply and increase the price. Normally these combinations are in restraint of free enterprise and create disillusionment out of which resentments and frustrations such as communism arise.

A Conservative Looks At Cooperatives

COMMUNISM

This refers to present day Sino-Soviet imperialism of both the Asian and European brands, and not the historic New Testament or present day (in some areas) non-violent attempts to form non-proprietary communistic communities.

COOPERATIVE

A cooperative is a voluntary organization of persons with a common interest, formed and operated along democratic lines for the purpose of supplying services at cost to its members and other patrons, who contribute both capital and business. The primary characteristics set forth in this definition are: voluntary service provided, democratic control by members, services at cost, member contributions of capital, and member patronage. It is not a tool of the government, but it is subject to the rules of law, as interpreted by the courts for this special type of business corporation.

This definition is the opposite of the word "cooperative" as used in the communist world where the cooperative is a subservient tool of the State. [Definition developed by Raymond J. Mischler, *Rocky Mountain Law Review* (June 1958), 383.]

CREDIT UNION

A credit union is an organization formed by a group of people who save their money together and make loans to each other for good purposes at low interest. Each credit union is an independent, nonprofit corporation, chartered and supervised by the government. The most significant single fact about a credit union is that the members own it. The credit union is a self-owned, self-help enterprise. [Definition from *Credit Union Yearbook* (International Headquarters, Filene

House, Madison, Wisconsin), Section II, p. 26.]

MUTUAL BUSINESS ORGANIZATION

A mutual business organization is slightly different from a cooperative in operation and voting rights but legally it falls into the family of cooperative nonprofit business organizations, such as chambers of commerce and farmer cooperatives which are covered in the same U.S. Statutes relating to tax exemption for nonprofit organizations.

NONPROFIT BUSINESS CORPORATION
(Sometimes called the nonprofit corporation.)

This is another phrase for a true cooperative. It operates under the same business principles and utilizes the same items as the profit and loss corporation: men, management, and material. This legal entity, however, is incorporated to serve its own member patrons at cost, under a prior agency contract to act for them in the securing of goods or services or marketing their products, returning to them any overcharges or delayed payments and assessing them for any undercharges or over-payments made to them by mistake.

PATRONAGE DIVIDEND

Patronage dividend means an amount paid to a patron, from corporate earnings, on the basis of patronage rather than investment. It includes (a) an amount paid out of earnings other than from business done with or for patrons, or (b) such amounts paid out of earnings from business done with patrons to whom no patronage refunds are paid, or to whom smaller amounts are paid, with respect to substantially identical transactions. [Definition developed by Dr. A. Ladru Jensen, Professor of Law, University of Utah.]

201

PATRONAGE REFUND   Patronage refund means an amount paid to a patron on the basis of quantity or value of business done with or for such patron, under an obligation of such cooperative organization, which obligation existed before the organization received the amount so paid, and which is determined by reference to the net patronage proceeds of the organization from business done with or for its patrons in whose favor such obligation exists. [Definition developed by Dr. A. Ladru Jensen, Professor of Law, University of Utah.]

PROFIT AND LOSS CORPORATION   These are corporate businesses whose aim is to make a profit for stockholders on the use of invested capital. Men, management, and materials are combined to develop a business to attract and keep trade with patrons who may or may not, but usually do, own stock in the company.

CROWNED DEMOCRACIES   Crowned democracies are those representative democracies that also have a hereditary king or monarch as the symbolic head of the government, with a prime minister exercising the executive function normally exercised by the president of democracies having no royal family. This will include such countries as the North Sea monarchies and Canada, Australia, New Zealand, Greece and Japan. They are the basic mainstay of the free world aside from the United States and one or two other non-monarchial representative democracies.

DEMOCRACY   By democracy is meant that combination of political theories and practices that has evolved into the type of government we have in the United States.

DIVIDEND

A dividend, as applied to a going concern, is a return on invested capital. It normally denotes that part of the earnings of a profit entity corporation declared by the Board of Directors to be paid to stockholders at a certain time.

ULTRA VIRES

This is a technical, legal term meaning beyond the scope of the corporation charter. It is also, on occasions, applicable in the nonprofit field because of the tendency that some cooperatives have of entering into some forms of business for which they do not have a charter or statutory right.

These appendices include reprints of materials that are pertinent to evaluating the place of the nonprofit organization in the capitalistic world.

APPENDIX 1

In 1945-46, I, together with Harvey Hedgepeth of the Mississippi Bar, the late Herbert R. Grossman of the Kentucky Bar, A. Ladru Jensen of the Utah Bar, and Edson Abel of the California Bar, as "lawyer friends of the court" individually or collectively, attended all the sittings of the Royal Inquiry of the Canadian Government concerning cooperatives.

Following one of the sessions, Herbert Grossman and I had a weighty informal discussion with a representative of a Canadian newspaper. The discussion centered on a statement by us to the effect that the Canadian Press and its companion, the Associated Press in the United States, were bona fide cooperatives. The newspaper gentleman doubted this statement and the discussion ended there.

A year later, I was at the Chateau Laurier in Ottawa, and it so happened that the day was my birthday, January 21. On returning to my room, I found fifty copies of *The Evening Citizen,* one of the leading papers of Ottawa, Canada, deposited on my bed, together with a note, "Happy Birthday—You were right."

Following is a feature article by Stephen Ford, which is one of the finest statements ever made by any writer concerning the need for, and operation of, a service cooperative cooperation—it is the story in the newspapers on my bed.

EXCITING STORY OF 5,000,000
WORDS A DAY

The logotype (CP) in the datelines of uncounted news stories is the emblem of a Canadian news commonwealth, built up in three decades from an idea to a million-dollar-a-year enterprise.

This enterprise—which sells nothing, makes no profits, declares no dividends—is The Canadian Press. Almost 30 years ago the original idea reached fruition in a Canadian-wide association of daily newspapers. Since then the CP has grown until Canadian papers are receiving what can fairly be termed the finest news service in the world. Newspapers of no other country carry an international news report so broad, so complete, so closely tuned to their needs.

The Canadian Press is the cooperative news-gathering and distributing association of Canadian daily papers. Some of the news it gathers itself, some of it comes from the outside by exchange arrangements, but most of the news it draws directly from the 90-odd newspapers (all but five of Canada's dailies) receiving wire news services in its membership. After sorting, rewriting and editing, The Canadian Press distributes this news supply back among its members (of whom more than 70 depend on it entirely for outside news) for display to the 10,000,000 daily newspaper readers in Canada. Thus The CP might also be called a clearing house. The fact that it rewrites much of the news supplied by its member papers and distributes it for them under the familiar (CP) logotype does not alter the definition.

Of the very essence of The CP is its 11,000-mile system of leased wires. Of the million dollars it spends yearly, one-sixth is for wire rentals alone. CP trunk circuits, leased from Canadian Pacific Communications, run up and down across the country from Glace Bay, N.S., to Nanaimo, B.C. Capillaries of provincial wires fan out the flow to newspapers off the main line. In Ontario alone 25 papers are served on 10 circuits out of Toronto. If the copy transmitted over the leased CP circuits were handled instead on a toll basis—press rate is a quarter-cent a word between Toronto and Montreal for instance—the cost would be a fabulous figure. On a day when the budget comes down at Ottawa or a world statesman makes a vital speech, The CP's 250 teleprinters may carry 5,000,000 words in 24 hours.

The Canadian Press does a business involving expenditure of a million dollars a year but it isn't in any list of commercial firms. It owns no buildings or property except the furniture and fixtures in its bureaux. The annual budget is figured out and met by lumping the general charges—such as wire rentals, salaries, etc.—and dividing them, city by city, where there is a member newspaper, on the basis of population. Where there are more than one paper in a city, the charge is divided equally between the members. The assessments may shift each year if the budget varies and they do change every 10 years when census figures are issued.

200,000 WORDS A DAY

Core of The CP's wire system is the head office at Toronto, where 30 editors and 20 traffic men handle eastern news for the West and western news for the East, watching the flow of copy for accuracy and style and for development of obscure but interesting angles.

The boiling brew of international news makes London and New York key points of extreme importance. Throughout the Second World War, the bureaux at London, New York and Toronto never closed and the busy teleprinters were never silent.

In New York, on the fifth floor of the ultra-modern Associated Press Building, seven CP men select with quick decision the news report that is then piped into Canada 24 hours a day, seven days a week. These editors with news sense sharpened by training in CP bureaux across Canada, blue-pencil some 200,000 words a day to the 86,000 words their outgoing circuit will carry at 60 words a minute. The CP editors at New York handle a flood of news that rattles into the office on eight teleprinters from three main sources—the output of the CP overseas staff based on London bureau; the complete world news report of The Associated Press (the co-operative of 1,400 United States newspapers which pool $16,500,000 a year to let it collect their news) ; and the world service of Reuters (owned by the newspapers of the United Kingdom, with London and provincial papers sharing 50-50).

STRONG LONDON STAFF

At the London Bureau, in the Lutyens-designed Press Association Building on Fleet street, another job of sifting is done by seven Canadian editors who have available the complete report of Press Association, the organization of the United Kingdom's dailies, and the Bureau staff's own output on parliament and other functions on events of special Canadian interest. Because London is ahead of Canada in time by four hours (in the Maritimes) to eight (at the Coast) it is not uncommon for a lengthy report of a parliamentary session at Westminster to be on the street in Canada before *The Times* is being sold in London.

Competent balanced reporting of Canada's part in the Second World War strengthened CP's reputation for accuracy and fairness in handling news. World beats on several of the conflict's top stories proved CP reporters the equal of any. They gave Canada a clear picture of the War's progress and told the rest of the world of Canada's part in it.

Across Canada are seven bureaux—Halifax, Montreal, Ottawa, Toronto, Winnipeg, Edmonton, Vancouver—with day and night staffs to keep the news-stream flowing, meantime adding to it the boiled-down news product of the respective regions.

The CP staff numbers more than 200, of whom 70 are teleprinter operators and mechanics. The rest are members of the editorial staff, mostly filing editors (who cut incoming copy to the capacity of their outgoing circuits and keep the best news constantly ahead) and rewrite men (who boil down the copy received from CP member newspapers). Virtually every filing editor or rewrite man has been a reporter—and they frequently go back on the street if a big story breaks on which The CP needs coverage direct to its wires rather than by way of the member paper office. Ottawa is the only bureau where reporters outnumber editors, seven of the 11 staff members covering parliament, government departments and the military services.

EMPIRE NEWS LEADER

From 1933 to the end of 1940, The CP was also Canada's national news service on the air. For those seven years it provided without remuneration and at considerable cost radio bulletins day and night to the Canadian Broadcasting Corporation and to individual stations. Effective Jan. 1, 1941, an agreement was concluded with CBC to provide the entire CP news service to be processed into radio news by the CBC staff.

When it gave news to the CBC free, CP scorned any link with radio advertising. But in 1941 CP members realized sponsored news had come to stay and voted to make news available for commercial use on the air—a direct reversal of previous policy.

In mid-1944 a CP subsidiary Press News Limited, began to process newspaper copy for radio use and pipe it into radio stations by teleprinter. Within five years Press News was serving two-thirds of Canada's private broadcasters on a coast-to-coast circuit operating 24 hours a day.

As the first co-operative news association in the Empire, The CP is leader in the movement for a co-operative Empire Press—a development still far in the future, though New Zealand, Australia and South Africa in recent years have established news associations along semi-co-operative lines. Two CP steps in the direction of Empire news co-operation are a service of world news provided by cable to British West Indies newspapers and the development of a cable-and-mail exchange of background news with other interested Dominions.

The history of co-operative news-gathering in Canada goes back 40 years to when the average small city daily was padded with boiler-plate and its world news was restricted to occasional and spasmodic bulletins supplied by the railway telegraph companies.

The first step in news co-operation was taken in 1937 when the Western Associated Press came into being in Winnipeg. It was founded by the Winnipeg publishers to meet an intolerable situation—control of news service to Canada by the railways. The Canadian Pacific Railway held the rights to The Associated Press for the Dominion, and collection of news in Ontario and Quebec was largely in the hands of the Great North Western Telegraph Company, a Grand Trunk affiliate. Its service was cheap but woefully poor—the papers had to take what they got.

BORN OF NEWS REVOLT

Formation of the W.A.P. was the first move in a newspaper revolt. It gathered support in the West and entered into direct competition with the C.P.R. Deprived of the Associated Press service, it obtained such connections as were available, and waged an uphill fight. Its members carried on loyally though they were getting what in some ways was an inferior news service at a cost much greater than that supplied by the C.P.R. to their competitor across the street. Meanwhile, there was general agreement among Canadian publishers that sooner or later they must establish their own news agency. In 1909 Maritime daily publishers founded the Eastern Press Association, based on the same ideal of co-operative news service.

The turning point came when the Western Associated Press appealed to the Railway Commission, which controlled telegraph rates, against the exorbitant rates charged by the CPR for transmission of WAP news as compared with the low rates charged for the CPR service. In the appeal, the daily publishers of Ontario and Quebec stood shoulder to shoulder with their western confreres. In 1910 the Railway Commission declared in favor of equal rates for all press matter. The fight was over. The CPR, in later years a staunch friend of The Canadian Press, recognized that it was out of its sphere in the news agency field and surrendered Associated Press rights in Canada to the Canadian daily newspapers.

NATIONAL UNITY SERVED

It was necessary to set up an organization to take over these rights and guarantee to The AP a return service of Canadian news. The establishment in 1911 of the Canadian Press Limited resulted. The ambition of its founders was to make it a truly national organization, but until 1917 it was merely a holding Company for the Canadian rights of The Associated Press. The WAP and EPA served newspapers in the West and the Maritimes. In Ontario and Quebec separate organizations were formed for morning and evening papers respectively. To some extent the four independent agencies exchanged the news of their territories, but the arrangement was loose, wasteful and cumbersome.

Barriers to a national agency were the broad, almost unpopulated, expanses separating the news organizations —without leased wires across these gaps there could be no united association and the cost was prohibitive. The gaps were three—Saint John to Montreal, Toronto to Winnipeg, and Calgary to Vancouver.

ONE PAPER, ONE VOTE

The Canadian Press is run by its general manager, directed by its 21-member board. Each member, large or small, has one vote in affairs of the association and in election of directors. The directors are elected annually by regions, three from the Maritimes, four from Quebec (including two representing French-language papers), six from Ontario, two each from the four western provinces. The directors elect annually a president, two vice-presidents and an honorary president. The president, vice-presidents and two directors are an executive committee to strike estimates and authorize interim extraordinary expenditures.

President of The CP is F. I. Ker of the Hamilton *Spectator*. Victor Sifton, Winnipeg *Free Press,* is First Vice-president, Herve Major, Montreal *La Presse,* Second Vice-president, and Senator W. Rupert Davies, Kinston *Whig-Standard,* Honorary President.

Directors are: H. P. Duchemin, Sydney *Post-Record;* R. J. Rankin, Halifax *Mail;* T. F. Drummie, Saint John *Telegraph-Journal;* A. F. Mercier, Quebec *L'Evenement-Journal;* A. J. West, Montreal *Star;* G. H. Carpenter, Montreal *Gazette;* George McCullagh, Toronto *Globe and Mail;* John Motz, Kitchener *Record;* Arthur R. Ford, London *Free Press;* Roy H. Thompson, Timmins *Press;* E. C. Whitehead, Brandon *Sun;* D. B. Rogers, Regina *Leader-Post;* Allan Holmes, Moose Jaw *Times-Herald;* Charles E. Campbell, Edmonton *Bulletin;* F. F. Payne, Nelson *News;* O. Leigh-Spencer, Vancouver *Province.*

The general manager is Gillis Purcell, who was named to the post in 1945 after 17 years with CP. Under him is a loyal and competent staff whose *esprit-de-corps* is remarked on wherever Canadian newspapermen gather. It is well known in the business that the CP man works longer under steadier pressure than the newspaperman on the individual paper—and for no more money—but he likes it.

APPENDIX 2

In 1957, Mr. Charles Taft, Chairman of the Department of the Churches and Economic Life of the National Council of Churches asked me to serve as Chairman of a Consultation which was to be held at Haverford College to explore the concern that churchmen should have in regard to cooperatives and mutual businesses.

This Consultation had been authorized as a result of a long series of discussions and studies of the general subject within the Department.

Some fifty men spent several days at Haverford examining the place of cooperatives and mutual businesses in a society of free people.

Never have I experienced more thoughtful consideration of a subject. While the conclusions were, and are, the expression of the men who participated in the discussions and do not represent a commitment on the part of the National Council or its member churches, they do represent a "landmark" study in this field and part of their conclusions are included in this Appendix as a valuable addition to this book.

A NEW LOOK AT COOPERATIVES AND MUTUAL BUSINESSES[1]
A Guide for Study and Discussion
(For use in church and other groups)
Compiled by Benson Y. Landis

---

[1]*This study and discussion guide is based largely on the report of a Consultation on the Churches and Cooperatives and Mutual Businesses, Haverford, Pa., 1957. The full text of the report from which the following are excerpted is available from the Department of the Churches and Economic Life of the National Council of Churches, 297 Fourth Avenue, New York, N. Y.*

A Conservative Looks At Cooperatives

Foreword

Foreword

It is hoped that this Study and Discussion Guide will receive wide reading among the clergy, the laity, and the general public. The Consultation on the Churches and Cooperatives and Mutual Businesses was a milestone on the road to clear thinking concerning these important parts of American business. The high caliber and breadth of knowledge of the participants resulted in a report which, as time goes on, will be of increasing importance.

Dr. Benson Y. Landis, who reported the findings of the Consultation and authored this Study Guide, has performed another valuable service. He is one of America's most discerning and renowned writers in this field covered by the Consultation.

This Guide should prove to be a valuable asset in making these conclusions easily available for discussion purposes.

Raymond W. Miller, Chairman
Consultation on the Churches and
Cooperatives and Mutual Businesses

Introduction

This Guide is prepared to aid in "re-examining Protestant thinking on the position and responsibility of the churches with respect to cooperatives and mutual businesses." It is another step in a process begun in 1957 with the holding of a consultation in which fifty persons invited by the Department of the Church and Economic Life of the National Council of Churches participated. The reports of the discussions of that group, whose members spoke only for themselves and were not delegates from church bodies, were published in *Information Service,* September 21, 1957. Portions of these reports are reprinted in this text as resource material for leaders or teachers, and members of discussion groups or classes. Use of the full text of the printed Report in connection with this Guide is recommended. Because of the limitations of time, cooperatives were considered at the Consultation more fully than mutual businesses.

The issues considered in this Guide are mainly those taken up by the Consultation. They are so arranged as to draw out the personal experience or reading of groups or classes, and to relate this experience or reading to that of others and to varied subject matter with respect to cooperatives and mutual businesses. A brief reading list is given and in the text references are made to specific titles.

The Guide begins with a consideration of the nature and extent of cooperatives and mutual businesses. Because credit unions are often organized within churches and other religious organizations, a section is devoted to these institutions. Then follow considerations of contributions and limitations, the relation to other forms of business, cooperatives in other lands and in relation to international relations and world peace, with a final section summing up the religious and ethical aspects.

The arrangement of this Guide is primarily such as to assist in an informal group discussion by young people or adults. The teacher of a class of young people or adults can adapt it to his purposes, and the organizer of a panel or a forum should find questions or data that will be helpful.

In many instances, a group or class within a church will find a person with experience in cooperatives and mutual businesses ready and willing to assist by supplying local information and experience or by welcoming persons wishing to visit an office or headquarters. Credit unions are now so widely organized in cities that someone with experience is nearby. In rural areas cooperatives and mutual businesses are extensive among farmers.

Session   *Nature and Extent of Cooperatives*
1   *and Mutual Businesses*[1]

"It seems clear," said participants in the Haverford Consultation on the Churches and Cooperatives and Mutual Businesses, "that there is no single motivation underlying the development of the many cooperative movements and experiments in mutual aid which have grown up

[1]*Other Sessions were on the following subjects: Credit Unions; Contributions and Limitations; Relation to Other Forms of Business; Cooperatives, Missions and World Peace; and Religious and Ethical Aspects.*

throughout the world in the past several centuries. Some have been founded upon grinding economic poverty and the natural impulse to overcome it with whatever tools are at hand. Some have grown up out of a desire on the part of responsible segments of the community to infuse an element of democratic control into rapidly expanding and centralizing systems. Still others reflect the concern of professing Christians eager to make all areas of life the stage upon which the drama of fellowship can be enacted."

The cooperative is a form of business enterprise which emphasizes voluntary collective action for the benefit of its members. There are numerous statements of principles available. One presented to the Consultation read in part: "Democratic control" (usually by means of one-man, one-vote); "limited returns on invested capital"; "operation at cost with sharing of benefits and savings among members in proportion to the volume each member transacts through the association." To these are often added: Open membership; political and religious neutrality; and cash trading. "The member stands in a three-fold relationship to his cooperative — member, patron, and investor."

APPENDIX 3

Although I am a member of the Methodist Church, since the summer of 1940 I have attended many sessions having to do with rural affairs called by the Roman Catholic Church both here and abroad. In 1949, jointly with Father Kevin O'Dwyer, S.J., I conducted and held some fifty meetings in the "barrios" of the Philippines concerning the place of co-operatives in the newly-formed Republic. In the subsequent years I have met many Roman Catholics, both priests and laity, who are vitally concerned in the positive part that the nonprofit corporation may play in developing a free democratic society.

In 1961 Pope John promulgated a Papal Encyclical entitled "Mater et Magistra." Because the nonprofit cooperative is discussed in this document, I asked Father James L. Vizzard, S.J., Director of the Washington Office of the National Catholic Rural Life Conference, to make a compilation of those statements in the encyclical which are relevant to cooperatives. The following are his excerpts:

Papal Encyclical

The cause of the cooperatives received emphatic high-level endorsement in Pope John XXIII's recent encyclical, "Christianity and Social Progress."[1] The following are some of the more significant passages of the encyclical which deal with cooperatives:

"It is not possible in economic affairs to determine in one formula all the measures that are more comfortable to the dignity of man, or are more suitable in developing in him a sense of responsibility. Nevertheless, our predecessor, . . . Pius XII, appropriately laid down certain norms of action: 'Small and medium-sized holdings in agriculture, in the arts and crafts, in commerce and in-

[1]*Latin title "Mater et Magistra." Available at National Catholic Welfare Conference, 1312 Massachusetts Avenue, N. W., Washington 5, D. C.*

217

dustry, should be safeguarded and fostered. Such enterprises should join together in cooperative societies in order that the services and benefits of large-scale enterprises will be available to them.' " (84)

"Wherefore, conformably to requirements of the common good and the state of technology . . . farm enterprises of family type should be safeguarded and fostered, as should also cooperatives that aim to complement and perfect such enterprises." (85)

"Moreover, the measures taken by the State on behalf of the craftsmen and members of cooperatives are also justified by the fact that [they] . . . are producers of genuine wealth, and contribute to the advance of civilization." (89)

"Accordingly, we paternally exhort our beloved sons . . . members of cooperatives throughout the world, that they fully realize the dignity of their role in society, since, by their work, the sense of responsibility and spirit of mutual aid can be daily more intensified among the citizenry, and the desire to work with dedication and originality be kept alive." (90)

"If a family-type farm is to survive, it must produce sufficient income to enable the family to live in decent comfort. To do this, it is very necessary that farmers be given special instructions, be kept constantly up-to-date and be supplied with technical assistance in their profession. It is also essential that they form a flourishing system of co-operatives and professional organizations." (143)

"It is Our opinion that farmers themselves as the interested parties ought to take the initiative and play an active role in promoting their own economic advancement, social progress and cultural betterment." (144)

"We wish to bestow well-deserved praise on Our sons in various parts of the world who are actively engaged in establishing and furthering cooperatives and other types of associations to the end that farm workers in every community may enjoy both an adequate share of economic blessings and a decent life." (148)

APPENDIX 4

Mr. John H. Heckman, Acting Director, International Cooperative Development Staff (A.I.D.) has had a long and distinguished career in cooperative development. For many years he was associated with the Farmer Cooperative Service of the U. S. Department of Agriculture and, as such, I observed his work in Europe and Latin America, as well as here in North America.

Included in this Appendix are two recent writings of his:

(1) "Achilles' Heels of Cooperation"—this report was prepared at the request of the Government of India and was printed in the official publication of the Ministry of Community Development and Cooperation. It dramatizes the basic requisites of cooperation. The report is being given wide attention by both government and nongovernment agencies. It was written after two years of experience, and Mr. Heckman is able to deal more effectively with some of the delicate Indian problems.

(2) The second item is a portion of a report which Mr. Heckman prepared on behalf of the Committee of Advisers on Cooperatives, of which I am a member, for the Director of the A.I.D. program. This statement condenses his many years of study and should become a vital part of the literature in the field of cooperative efforts.

ACHILLES' HEELS OF COOPERATION
By JOHN H. HECKMAN

A strange subject you may ask. Cooperatives are modern and real, while Achilles is ancient and mythological. But some of our best lessons come from the most unexpected and unconventional teachers. So what can the cooperatives learn from Achilles?

219

A Conservative Looks At Cooperatives

The first lesson might be that they are vulnerable to fatal attacks. The protection of the magic armour and the bath in the River Styx enabled Achilles to survive many battles and to slay Hector. But the vulnerable heel was finally pierced by the avenging arrow of Paris. Protected, guided and nurtured by benevolent governments and philanthropic well-wishers, cooperatives may survive and seemingly prosper as did Achilles. But beyond this sheltering armour and the symbolic bath do the cooperatives have areas exposed to the arrows of modern economic and social descendants of Paris?

The assumption in our title implies that there are such and that there are more than one. The proportion of cooperatives in many areas with audit classifications of D and E indicate some modern arrows are piercing cooperative heels. Further evidence is the fact that the Working Group on Cooperative Development during the Third Five Year Plan estimates that 60,000 or 30 per cent of the 2 lakhs societies in 1960-61 need revitalizing. Thus some modern successors of the Trojan Archer have been doing some sharp shooting at the unarmoured cooperative heels. The question is how to build a super armour to protect them?

ULTIMATE OBJECTIVE

Before an armour can be built to protect the sensitive cooperative heels, it is necessary to thoroughly understand the person who will wear it. Just what is a cooperative? Of course, there are many definitions. But for our purpose, let's assume that "cooperatives are socio-economic democracies owned and controlled by their member-patrons and designed to perform needed services for them." The 'socio' is placed first in the definition as cooperatives do have a social responsibility. In some instances the social out-weighs the economic. But there is no income from social services. They mainly involve outgo. Government and other forms of assistance for both social and economic functions may be extended to advantage during the developing years of a cooperative. But the ultimate objective should be for the cooperatives to stand alone as independent democracies. Therefore, it is necessary for them first to be economic successes in order to take advantage of their social opportunities.

This resolves our question of how to make them an economic success. Cooperatives are composed of many people. This results in many involved processes. So it is easy to confuse the details with the underlying principles. But we said in our definition that cooperatives were designed to perform needed services for their members. Isn't that the purpose of any business? If so, do not the same factors that affect success in any business also affect cooperatives? In other words, are not the cooperatives interested in achieving the same results for their member-owners that an individual man wishes to achieve for his business? The difference being that many people are involved in the cooperative and only one in the other business. But suppose that one man operated a business as large as the cooperative. Both his social and economic objectives would likely be different, which is the basis for cooperatives. But as joint-owners of a business enterprise, are not the members of a cooperative interested in achieving the same benefits from services that would an individual owner if he owned the entire enterprise? If so, what would be the basic factor for its success?

BASIC UNDERSTANDING

With this understanding, what are the factors that assure a successful business? Without hesitation, I believe we would agree that the first requisite is to understand it. It is clearly impossible to plan for and conduct a business successfully that the owner does not understand. He must know its objective, practical means of achieving them, sources and costs of the same services from competitors and many other things. Without this knowledge, the business will wander aimlessly like a helmless ship and finally founder on the reefs of confusion.

Multiply the one owner, by many member-owners and you have the cooperative. Each member-owner has the same basic interest in his portion of the cooperative as the man who owns a business of the same size. Also the same interest the member had in the service before he joined the cooperative and it was performed in his

221

own home or at his farm. There the service was carefully nurtured with the interest and pride of ownership. An unproductive plot of land was carefully improved, because of the pride in and rewards of ownership. Yet what about the cooperative of which he is a member and part-owner? Without thought of nurturing it as he did his field if it needs improving, many times he will casually obtain his services elsewhere. Why the difference? He knows that the field is his, but he is not so sure about the cooperative, even if the cooperative Instructor did tell him so. He must be further convinced, and the basic success of the cooperative depends upon his conviction. This gives rise to the statement, that "cooperatives, like all democracies thrive in direct proportion to the understanding of their members." Thus, the lack of basic understanding among members, may be listed as the first vulnerable cooperative heel, not covered by conventional armour.

An illustration or two will be given of the advantage of forging an armour of understanding among the members of cooperatives. In my own country, a large regional cooperative was faced with a shortage of oil. The need could be met by a refinery owned by the cooperative. But refineries cost a great deal of money. The managing committee provided for the need for oil and a refinery as a possible solution, to be discussed at small community meetings throughout the areas served by the cooperative. By the time the community meetings were completed, not only had the decision regarding need been reached but the money to build the refinery had been subscribed. The armour of understanding had proved effective as arrows of doubt and hesitation filled the air. In sharp contrast, the managing committee of another large regional cooperative, quickly reached the decision to build a facility and sent the canvassers to the members to raise the required capital. Unshielded by the armour of understanding the members fell victims to the poisoned darts of doubt and suspicion. As a result the capital was never raised.

A nearer example is the experience of trainees at our Basic Instructors' Training Centre with nearby villagers. One of the "Learning by Doing" portions of the course is to conduct a series of practice programmes in the villages. The trainees of the first course went out with well

222

prepared discussions on the Principles and Practices of Cooperation. But the villagers did not understand their motives and did not see the discussions as answers to their problems. As a result the trainees were ridiculed and accomplished little. Succeeding classes have sent representatives to the village in advance to confer with representative villagers on conditions and problems in the village. Against this background of information, programmes were prepared using the same principles and practices as the earlier class. But they were woven around problems the people themselves had selected and considered important. Thus they were real, the people understood them and felt a part of them. Again in contrast, these trainees had a good reception and are consistently invited back for extra meetings. Both illustrations involve the same communities, the same general subject matter and the same type of class. The difference—the armour of understanding.

More illustrations are available, but we should hasten back and investigate the second heel. Recall our title is plural. So we'll return to the individual business whose operations are as large as the cooperative. We have said that it is necessary for the owner to thoroughly understand the business in order to make it effective. In like manner it is necessary for the many joint owners of the cooperative to understand their business. But in addition to thoroughly understanding a business, in order to assure sound objectives, something further must be done. Even though guided by sound objectives based on complete understanding, isn't efficient management necessary to complete success?

EFFICIENT MANAGEMENT

Here we find the second unprotected heel that cooperative armour frequently does not cover. As mentioned, while cooperatives are socio-economic, they must first be economic successes before they can perform social services. So, as in any business, the understanding of the members must be accompanied by efficient management. Management is much broader than its tools, namely, production, accounting, financing and sales with their many sub-divisions. It is the combining of these tools into a compact

223

unit which results in black ink instead of red ink, and efficient, competitive and adapted services.

This establishes the second vulnerable heel of cooperatives. The first is membership understanding. The second is capable and competitive management. It is a matter of conjecture how many of the D and E cooperatives or what proportion of the 60,000 societies which the Working Group feels need revitalizing, are affected by these vulnerable heels. But it's safe to assume many.

It is also well to remember that Thetis, the mother of Achilles just took him by one heel when dipping him into the River Styx to achieve his protection. Also that the armour served him well through many hazards. But that the poisoned arrow of Paris finally pierced the one unprotected area and laid him low. Evidently, the mother of cooperation found him a more lusty infant. Thus it was necessary for her to take him by both heels when she plunged him into the protective waters. So as compared to Achilles, he is doubly vulnerable. Thus the armour of supervision, guidance, benevolence and ideology are necessary, helpful, and will give protection and win some battles. But if the heels of membership understanding and management are left exposed, sooner or later the cooperative will fall victim to the arrows of modern Paris,—doubt, suspicion and inefficiency.

COOPERATIVES IN DEVELOPING COUNTRIES

By John H. Heckman

Cooperatives have a vital place in the economic area of this country. But they have a far greater role in the economic progress of developing countries. In addition, there are other opportunities in developing countries that are not so evident in the United States. In this country, protective laws and effective competition are assuring factors of quality, ethics and adapted services. In developing countries, either or both of these may be lacking. Cooperatives have an opportunity to bridge this gap.

Cooperatives also have two additional opportunities in developing countries. These are: one, to stimulate the pride and stability that goes with the feeling of ownership and two, to serve as laboratories of democracy.

The magic word "mine" is a powerful stimulus. It causes houses to be painted, streets to be paved, fields to become more productive, children to be educated and battles to be won. We minimize it here when some property owned is taken for granted. Not so with the peasant, land-starved for centuries, or the shifting part-time laborer. To both a bicycle may be an out-of-reach luxury. To these people, the feeling of ownership and belonging which goes with their cooperative can be a strong stabilizing ballast to citizenship.

Cooperatives are economic and social democracies and grass roots democracies at that. The principles of democracies are the same whether political, social or economic. A country covered with local cooperatives and members who are understanding owners has never feared revolutions and military coups.

APPENDIX 5

The continuing need for the nonprofit corporation to act as a "business agent" for the individual is dramatically demonstrated in the following reprint from Toronto's *The Financial Post*, March 3, 1963.

Cooperation is definitely based upon continuing education. In a mobile society such as is possible in the free world, those who believe in cooperative effort must realize that the job is never done. Cooperative education is definitely for those with economic problems that they cannot solve alone.

BETTER MARKETING KEY
ESKIMO CO-OPS AGREE

By AUDREY GILL

Frobisher Bay—Canada's Eskimos are catching up with modern business methods: last week they even held a convention.

Delegates from 17 Eskimo co-operatives from all over the Arctic came to Frobisher to discuss their business problems and opportunities.

For many it was the first time they had traveled more than a few miles away from their own communities. They came from as far west as Aklavik (2,000 miles from Frobisher), near the Yukon border and as far east as Port Burwell at the tip of the eastern mainland. The most northern representative came from Grise Fiord, 1,500 miles north of Frobisher.

The key points brought out:
• The need for a central marketing agency in the south.
• A federation of all Eskimo co-ops.

When the meeting ended, the delegates returned home to discuss these proposals with their co-op members. Approval from all 500 members of the Arctic co-ops has to be obtained before these agencies can be set up.

The Department of Northern Affairs has been selling

Eskimo handicrafts and has arranged for the distribution of Arctic char in the south. The Cape Dorset co-op has handled all its own sales of prints for the last two years, and with great success.

Both Ottawa and the Eskimos feel they should get the co-ops on to a firm commercial basis as soon as is practical. Ottawa wants them to learn about and handle their own marketing: the co-ops would have to finance a southern agency.

The co-ops have been established to provide the Eskimos with a source of cash income, to improve methods of local resource harvesting and to give the Eskimos financial and emotional involvement in their own development. The department gives them assistance in management, accounting and loans for equipment.

Specialists are provided by the department to supervise the operations and train the Eskimos in techniques of operating commercial fisheries, logging and milling projects, handicraft and graphic art production, and retail stores. The specialist acts as an overseer—at the same time training them to get along without him. As the people become able to manage these projects on their own, the specialist's supervision is withdrawn.

Eventually all government assistance is withdrawn. One of the most serious of the problems to be solved; lack of formal education. Especially in the eastern Arctic, few adult Eskimos can read or write English so it probably will be a generation before all aspects of co-op ownership and management can be handled exclusively by the Eskimos themselves.

At the moment all the co-ops appoint a white man as secretary-treasurer. He is usually a northern administrator, a Mountie or a missionary.

Last year 16 co-ops between them did about $500,000 worth of business. Officials expect it to reach $1 million this year. The 500 members made about $200,000 in direct payments.

The Cape Dorset co-op, which is the largest in membership and sales, grossed $176,300 in the fiscal year to March 62. Of that, graphic arts and crafts accounted for $123,800 and the retail store brought in $40,900. The balance was from the tourist camp. This co-op now has a reserve fund of $50,000.

All the fishing co-ops now have freezers on a rental-purchase basis with Northern Affairs. The department also will lend up to $50,000 for 10 years at 5% to the co-ops from the Eskimo Loan Fund. There never has been a defaulter.

The Arctic char fisheries have been very successful. Approximately 200,000 lb. probably will be taken this year and the potential is much bigger. Most of it is sold frozen in southern Canada and the U. S. for about $1.25 lb. The Chimo fishery flies its daily catch to a fish broker in Montreal on *Nordair's* regular flight. The first overseas shipment of char went to Holland this week.

One of the newest co-ops is Sisi (Bear's Lair) at Frobisher Bay. Here the members got together and built 15 houses for themselves. Officials hope plans will go forward for more houses this summer.

The Eskimos bought pre-fabricated houses which cost $4,637, landed in Frobisher. Each member obtained a $3,500 loan from the Eskimo Loan Fund, received a $1,000 federal housing subsidy and paid $137 downpayment in cash. The houses are some of the best for Eskimos in the North.

Northern Affairs is investigating the possibilities of fish canning plants. A pilot cannery will be built this summer at Bernheimer Bay, Keewatin. There is no community there but Eskimos will be moved in for the summer work. Officials believe there is a substantial market for canned char in the Eskimos' own retail stores, as well as in the south.

Government officials were pleased by the success of the conference. "In four years some have come to a point where they can control their own affairs, except in marketing", Don Snowden says. He was chairman of the conference and is chief of the department's industrial division.

Most of the delegates agreed with the representatives from Coppermine who said they definitely need a sales agency in the south. He said the co-op used to depend on a little tourist trade during the summer and DEW-Line trade during the winter. Now the co-op has expanded so much it can't keep going on such a small volume.

INDEX

231

Human engineering, basic principles of, 128-129
Hynes, Mrs. Emerson, 132

Income Tax—
    double taxation of corporate dividends, 152-154
    payment by cooperatives, 133-136, 142-144
India—
    "Achilles' Heels of Cooperation," report on cooperatives in, 219-224
    conditions which led to organization of credit unions, 28-30, 113
    Constitution provision favoring cooperatives, 114
    Cooperative League of the U. S. A. operations in, 65
    cooperatives in—
        face great public relation task, 121
        operated by government, 116-117, 120-121
        lack of credit problems in, 114-115
        marketing cooperatives a necessity, 115-116
        organization of fishing cooperative, in Calcutta, 67-68
        panchayats in, defined, 112-113
    Report on Small Industries in India, excerpts from, 113-121
    Reserve Bank of, and cooperatives, 115, 118, 120
Indian cooperatives, 92
Inducing Cooperative Effort in Asia, 106-108
Internal Revenue—
    Act of 1951, provisions of, 134, 154
    Act of 1962, provisions of, 154
    "Federal Tax Issues in 1955," 73
    provisions of Subchapter S of Code, 152

ruling as to patronage refunds, 134
rulings on taxing retained patron equities, 43
International Conference on The Church and Rural Life, 32
International Federation of Agricultural Producers—
    interest in cooperatives, 101, 102, 103
    relationship with FAO on cooperatives, 101-105
    ways it can develop cooperatives, 104
Insurance, mutual association for, 96
Introducing the Author, 195-198
Ireland, cooperatives—communism in, 58
Irrigation companies (mutual) in U.S., 97
Israel, Kibbutz in, 78-79
Italy—
    banks for cooperatives organized, 69
    cooperatives, communism in, 58, 69

Jamaica, Credit Union developed at Kingston, 112
Japan—
    Cooperatives Helped Build Stable, 63
    cooperatives in, supported by MacArthur administration, 58, 107
    land reform in, 107
    per capita income in, 108
    35,000 rural cooperatives organized in, 63
Jensen, Dr. A. Ladru—
    American Bar Association report on cooperatives (quoted), 141-142
    appreciation to, 194

247 Fed. 183 (D. Ore. 1917), 253 Fed. 848 (D. Ore. 1918), 97

Dickinson v. Board of Trade, 114 Ill. A. 295 (1904), 91

Dodge v. Ford Motor Co., 204 Mich. 458, 170 N. W. 668 (1919), 89

Eisner v. McCumber, 252 U. S. 189 (1920), 151

Garkane Power Co. v. Public Service Commission, 98 Utah 466, 100 P. 2d 571 (1940), 97

Inland Empire Rural Electrification v. Dept. of Public Service of Washington, 199 Wash. 527, 92 P. 2d 258 (1939), 97

James v. United States. 366 U.S. 213, 1961, 154

McClure v. Cooperative Elevator & Supply Co. 103 Kan. 91, 181 Pac. 573 (1919), 90

Minister of National Revenue v. Stanley Mutual Fire Insurance Company, (Supreme Court of Canada), 137-138

New York Life Insurance Co. v. Styles (Surveyor of Taxes), decision by British House of Lords, 136-137, 138, 155

Railway Express Agency v. Commissioner of Internal Revenue, 169 F. 2d. 193 (1948) affirming 8 T. C. 991, 141

Southern California Edison Co. v. Railroad Commission of California, 194 Cal. 757, 230 Pac. 661 (1924), 97

State v. Willett, 171 Ind. 296, 86 N. E. 68 (1908), 90

Tidewater Coal Exchange, 13 Del. Ch. 195, 116 Atl. 898 (1922), 90

United States v. Jellico Mountain Coal & Coke Co., 46 Fed. 432 (1891), 146-147

U. S. v. Maryland and Virginia Milk Producers Assn., 362 U. S. 458, 1960, 145, 148

U. S. Board of Tax Appeals, Appeal of Paducah and Illinois Railroad Company, 138-139

White v. Brownell, 3 Abb. Pr. (N. S.) [N. Y.] 318 (1868) aff'd 2 Daly 329, 91

Lincoln, Murray—
first president of CARE, 86
helped organize CARE, 58
inspired bank for cooperatives in Italy, 69
interest in cooperatives in Japan, 63
Vice President in Charge of Revolution, 63, 152

"Little man," opportunity through cooperatives, 54, 57, 59, 60

Magic of Cooperative Effort, The, 28-31

Malnutrition, 44

Man—
credit union permits small to be self-respecting, 30
race between, and starvation, 106
what he wants in life, 52-53

Management—
defects in policies of, 184-185
member attitude toward, 179-181
must meet business world on equal terms, 166
research its most vital tool, 188-191

Manager—
desirable characteristics of a, 164, 166-167
employing expert, 184
must recognize need for research, 189
responsibilities of, 166-167

Marketing cooperatives, reputation for grading quality, 169

Markham, Edwin, "The Man with
the Hoe," 191-192
Marx, Karl—
and monopoly capitalism, 54
Code of, opposed to Code of
Christ, 64
See *also* Communism.
Massachusetts—
"cooperative banks," defined, 96
first credit union law, 95
"Mater et Magistra," Papal Encyclical, mentions cooperatives,
217-218
Mehta, R. S. (quoted), 79
Member education, importance of,
179
Members—
may give consent to loan patronage dividends to cooperative,
144
suspicions of, toward management, 180
Membership—
must be adequate to support cooperative, 177
should be consulted about changes, 161
should be kept informed, 168
family should be considered as
unit, 161-162
solicitation, warnings as to, 170
Mergers, *See* Consolidations.
Mesopotamia, loss of liberty, 62
Miller, David W.—
appreciation to, 194
director, Farmers Mutual Insurance Co., 85
Miller, Raymond W.—
and Grossman, Herbert R., "The
Nonprofit Corporation or Association in the Non-Agricul-
tural Field," 88
and Jensen, A. Ladru, "Failures
of Farmers' Cooperatives," 175

"The Nonprofit Corporation or
Association in the Nonagricultural Field," 141
Can Capitalism Compete? 20, 51
Miller, Robert W., appreciation to,
193
Minnesota, University of, study of
poultry producers cooperative,
178
Mischler, Raymond J.—
appreciation to, 193
"Current Legal Developments Affecting Farmer Cooperatives,"
148
"Legal Phases of Farmer Cooperatives," 133
Missionary—
awakened poor to vision of better
life, 67
role and influence of American
Christian, 34
Municipal electric systems, 149
Mutual insurance associations, 96

Nashville Coal Exchange, 146-147
National Catholic Rural Life Con-
ference, report on cooperatives,
41
National Council of Churches, con-
sultation on cooperatives and
mutual businesses, 40-41
National Council of Farmer Coop-
eratives, resolution opposing
taxes upon dividends, 151
National Farm Board, 16
National Geographic Society, 80,
82-83
National Grange, resolution oppos-
ing taxes upon dividends, 151
National Press Club, 85
National Society of Accountants for
Cooperatives, 162
Nationwide Mutual Insurance Co.,
84
Negro, recognition of, in India
cooperative program, 65